How to Measure Digital Marketing

Metrics for assessing impact and designing success

How to Measure Digital Marketing

Laurent Florès

palgrave
macmillan

First published 2014 by
PALGRAVE MACMILLAN

Palgrave Macmillan in the UK is an imprint of Macmillan Publishers Limited, registered in England, company number 785998, of Houndmills, Basingstoke, Hampshire RG21 6XS.

Palgrave Macmillan in the US is a division of St Martin's Press LLC, 175 Fifth Avenue, New York, NY 10010.

Palgrave Macmillan is the global academic imprint of the above companies and has companies and representatives throughout the world.

Palgrave® and Macmillan® are registered trademarks in the United States, the United Kingdom, Europe and other countries

ISBN: 978–1–137–34068–9 hardback

This book is printed on paper suitable for recycling and made from fully managed and sustained forest sources. Logging, pulping and manufacturing processes are expected to conform to the environmental regulations of the country of origin.

A catalogue record for this book is available from the British Library.

A catalog record for this book is available from the Library of Congress.

Typeset by Aardvark Editorial Limited, Metfield, Suffolk.

Contents

Part 3 Digital marketing in the service of brand and business development ╱ **191**

List of figures

List of tables

Preface

> You cannot manage what you cannot measure. What gets measured, gets done!

The aim of this book is to define the basis of a common language among the various stakeholders in digital marketing by measuring its effectiveness or ROI (return on investment).

More than 15 years' experience in this field shows that very often certain things are not included, simply because the different market participants – media agencies, media networks, interactive agencies, advertisers, research firms – do not speak the same "language" and do not attribute the same meaning to the words, expressions, and other jargon used by Internet specialists.

No doubt the technical nature of the medium, first used and popularized by technicians (the famous "geeks"), is largely to blame, but it does not explain everything. Indeed, until quite recently (less than two to five years ago at most, depending on the region or country), advertisers willingly delegated the management of their digital marketing to their agencies. The more well-informed brands tried to work with online agencies, while others saw the Internet as simply "another medium" and accordingly assigned its management to their regular advertising agency. After all, since Internet expenditure only accounted for less than 5% of total media spending, what was the point of organizing differently and conceiving of its marketing in another way? But the inflection point has now been reached where Internet investment alone exceeds the threshold of 10% of total media spending. In France, for example, this threshold was passed in 2010, with Internet expenditure accounting for 12% of all cross-media spending.[1] Some countries, such as England and the USA, reached the inflection point much earlier, since today digital advertising investment already stands at around 20% of total media spending by advertisers.

In fact, recent estimates from industry analyst eMarketer[2] show that digital advertising expenditure worldwide "passed the $100 billion mark for the first time in 2012 … and will increase by a further 15.1% in 2013 to $118.4 billion" (Table 1.1).

> That will put worldwide digital ad spending levels – including online and mobile advertising spending, other than messaging-based formats – at 21.7% of the total amount spent on ads in all media this year, and on track to account for more than one-quarter of all ad spending by 2016. North America accounts for the greatest share of all digital ad spending, at 39% as of the end of 2012. As emerging markets in Asia-Pacific and Latin America up spending, however, North America and second-place Western Europe will slightly lose share throughout the forecast period. By 2016, 36.7% of spending will come from North America, and 23.7% from Western Europe. By then, Asia-Pacific will contribute 29.8% of all digital ad spend in the world.[2]

As a percentage of total ad spending, Western Europe's digital spending is slightly ahead of North America's, with 24.9% this year as against 24.6%. Asia-Pacific is not far behind, although in the Middle East and Africa, the region with the smallest percentage, just 7% of all advertising dollars go to digital media. eMarketer expects this figure to nearly double by 2016, although the region will still lag far behind the near 30% of ad spending devoted to digital in Western Europe and North America.

Over and above digital expenditure alone, nine out of every ten advertisers involved in "cross-media" investment (two-thirds of all advertisers) include the Internet in their media plan. From now on,

TABLE 1.1 Digital ad spending growth worldwide, by region and country, 2011–16

	2011 (%)	2012 (%)	2013 (%)	2014 (%)	2015 (%)	2016 (%)
Middle East and Africa	**55.8**	**47.9**	**47.4**	**38.5**	**30.0**	**26.5**
Latin America	**34.0**	**37.0**	**23.0**	**28.0**	**18.0**	**16.0**
Brazil	30.0	40.2	20.0	28.0	15.0	14.2
Argentina	90.0	40.0	30.0	32.0	22.0	18.0
Mexico	40.3	34.6	32.1	30.8	22.4	19.2
Other	20.1	26.2	20.5	21.8	21.7	17.5
Asia-Pacific	**23.1**	**25.0**	**19.0**	**16.0**	**14.0**	**13.0**
Indonesia	50.0	55.0	70.0	75.0	72.0	66.0
India	40.0	39.6	33.0	30.0	26.0	24.0
China*	43.2	39.0	30.0	27.0	21.0	19.0
Australia	13.9	14.3	13.6	11.0	9.0	7.8
Japan	8.0	12.5	9.0	7.5	6.0	5.3
South Korea	11.0	9.5	8.0	7.5	6.0	5.5
Other	72.4	54.5	28.7	15.9	15.8	12.7
Eastern Europe	**38.4**	**18.9**	**17.3**	**15.5**	**13.0**	**9.0**
Russia	53.7	34.0	24.0	18.0	13.0	10.0
Other	28.5	7.3	10.9	12.8	13.0	7.9
North America	**21.5**	**16.6**	**13.8**	**12.4**	**9.0**	**6.8**
USA	21.9	16.8	14.0	12.5	8.8	6.4
Canada	17.1	13.5	11.7	11.8	12.1	11.1
Western Europe	**13.9**	**10.6**	**11.0**	**10.0**	**7.4**	**6.6**
Finland	8.2	17.0	12.0	7.0	6.0	4.0
UK	16.8	14.0	10.0	11.0	8.0	7.0
Sweden	14.0	11.0	8.0	6.0	5.5	5.0
Germany	11.0	10.0	12.0	10.0	6.0	5.3
Italy	16.0	9.0	14.0	13.0	12.0	11.0
France	11.4	8.0	11.0	9.0	7.0	6.0
Norway	10.6	7.0	9.0	8.0	7.0	6.0
Denmark	16.0	6.0	9.0	8.0	7.0	7.0
Netherlands	11.9	6.0	8.0	7.0	7.0	6.0
Spain	12.6	–1.0	11.5	12.5	9.5	8.5
Other	15.8	15.0	13.7	9.5	6.1	5.9
Worldwide	**20.6**	**17.8**	**15.1**	**13.7**	**10.8**	**9.3**

Note: Includes advertising that appears on desktop and laptop computers as well as mobile phones and tablets, and includes all the various formats of advertising on those platforms; excludes SMS, MMS and P2P message-based advertising; *excludes Hong Kong.

Source: eMarketer, December 2012.[2]

there is no doubt that digital will become increasingly important, even if investment has yet to catch up with people's consumption practices (see Table 1.2).

TABLE 1.2 Daily time per medium (US adults) and share of media investment

	Media consumption (%)	Share of media investment (%)
Magazines	3.3	10.6
Newspapers	4.9	16.5
Mobile	8.1	0.5
Radio	15.6	11
Internet	25.2	18.7
TV	42.9	42.7

Source: Adapted from *eMarketer*.[2]

All this makes clear the bright future that digital has ahead it, even without taking full account of mobile Internet, which is growing exponentially. For advertisers, it is therefore essential to invest ever more in the Internet and in digital media in general, to the point where industry expert analyst Forrester[3] recently acknowledged that "'Digital marketing' is to become just 'marketing' in 2013," as all marketers' output will become "inherently digital" over the coming months. The question of the measurement and effectiveness of investment then becomes central, and essential for structuring, perpetuating, and optimizing marketing campaigns. But nothing is simple. Indeed, paradoxically, the medium that wants to be the "most measurable"[4] is still often difficult to measure and evaluate, and advertisers have great difficulty determining its impact on sales and, more generally, its contribution to the marketing chain and therefore the return on investment (ROI).

Before discussing this last point more thoroughly, it seems important, as mentioned above, to define certain key concepts that can provide a better understanding of the issues by all stakeholders: advertisers, online agencies, media agencies, state-owned media and research companies. This common language will necessarily promote exchanges and the attainment of shared objectives. This is the subject of Chapter 1.

Notes

1 SRI/IAB Study 2010.
2 eMarketer (2013) "Digital to account for one in five ad dollars," January 9, www.emarketer.com/Article/Digital-Account-One-Five-Ad-Dollars/1009592.
3 O'Reilly, L. (2013) "'Digital marketing' to become just 'marketing' in 2013," January 9, www.marketingweek.co.uk/news/digital-marketing-to-become-just-marketing-in-2013/4005302.article.
4 The pioneers of the Internet, and in particular media agencies, widely claimed that "on the Internet one could measure everything." But reality is very different. A lot can be "counted," but counting is not measuring. We will return to this point in Chapter 1.

Acknowledgments

A book is similar to a long journey. My journey started back in 2000 with my friend, "brother," and partner, Hemen Patel, when the two of us built CRM Metrix from scratch, in the surroundings of Chicago. Yes, it was our Amercian "dream." So, thank you Hemen, thank you Guillaume; the rest is history now.

This book is a product of my life experience measuring and understanding digital media. Along the way I have made great friends, worked for top brands and clients around the world, taught great students, and met inspiring academic colleagues. You have all helped me to grow and cultivate a passion for measuring digital marketing and marketing as a whole. It would be difficult to mention everyone here, so I simply want to dedicate this book to all of you, and I want to thank you sincerely for this wonderful journey. It's probably time for me to start another adventure now, and I know that I can trust my family and close friends to support me through it. "Palomaben," sailing through the past 13 years has been rich in all senses and I am sure that the next 50 years will be just as exciting. It ultimately comes down to us to make sure that they are! So, wish me "bon voyage!"

I would like to acknowledge and thank these companies for allowing me to incorporate some of their data, figures, and images into this book. These include:

eMarketer, Inc., Forrester Research Inc., Denoix, Pearson Education Limited, KISSmetrics (blog.kissmetrics.com), Google Inc., CRM Metrix, P&G France,

MetrixLab, comScore AdEffx and dunnhumby USA, Media TouchPoint, Alexa Internet, Berlin-en-ligne, Flyertalk.com, Semiocast, Crop Media, Appian Analytics (Global Market Insite), and GBS Decision Cockpits.

Table 2.2: Original source: *Marketing and the Bottom Line* (2000), Tim Ambler, Pearson Education Limited. Author saw it in: Shaw, R. and Merrick, D. (2005) *Marketing Payback*, Financial Times/Prentice Hall.

Figure 3.4, 4.4, and 5.13: Google and the Google logo are registered trademarks of Google Inc., used with permission.

Figure 5.3: © 2010, Alexa Internet (www.alexa.com).

I would also like to give my sincere thanks to Dunod, who made French rights available for this English translation.

part 1

Devising a measure of effectiveness applicable to digital marketing

Specific, interactive and "always on," digital marketing imposes a new order on all market actors – advertisers, media agencies, advertising agencies, and research institutes. In this perspective, it is important to grasp its characteristics and potential, and to do so upstream and downstream of the marketing strategy, from the development of awareness and the image of a brand through to the acquisition of new customers and/or the retention of existing customers. Such are the marketing objectives that dictate the choice of metrics and key performance indicators (KPIs) needed to measure the effectiveness of digital marketing.

1

Definitions of and actors involved in digital marketing's return on investment

Executive summary

- The emergence of the Internet – a wholly new medium – and its implications are probably the biggest change that marketing has faced since World War II. It is no longer just a fad, but a truly new order.

- The effectiveness and return on investment (ROI) of digital marketing are often difficult to assess, although in theory, they are highly quantifiable. Counting is not the same thing as measuring, and therein lies the great paradox of digital.

- All the stakeholders in the digital ecosystem must agree to establish a common language and a set of effectiveness metrics understood by everyone – the sustainability of digital marketing depends on this.

Defining digital marketing

The term "digital marketing" appeared only recently in the world of professional marketing and communication. It refers to the promotion of products and brands among consumers, through the use of all digital media and contact points.

Although digital marketing has many similarities with Internet marketing, it goes beyond it, since it frees itself from the Internet's single point of contact and accesses all so-called "digital media," including, for example, mobile telephony (SMS or applications) and interactive television, as the communication channel. The term "digital marketing" therefore seeks to bring together all the interactive digital tools at the service of marketers for promoting products and services, while seeking to develop more direct and personalized relationships with consumers.

An advanced form of marketing

Far from following a fashion, with marketing and advertising becoming increasingly interactive, digital marketing covers ever more techniques and methods generally derived from traditional marketing, for example direct marketing, since it can communicate individually with a target but in a digital way. At present, its role is also tending to expand and go beyond simply the "promotion" of marketing products to include customer marketing or *consumer commitment*, that is, making available various ways of serving customers so as to maintain and develop the relationship, loyalty, and commitment of certain customers in the co-creation or co-promotion of offerings.[1]

In the coming years, marketing will be digital or nothing. Capable not only of selling but also creating loyalty and even "fanaticizing" customer relationships (in the Facebook sense), with digital marketing, the marketing of "the good" and "the link" are equally important, complementary, and essential for attracting and retaining increasingly "connected" consumers and for ever more fragmented media uses.

Toward a mix of push and pull

Marketing specialists are no doubt familiar with the expressions "push" and "pull." They refer to communication actions implemented by brands which, in the case of push, will enable them to reach their targets. Whatever the goals set – to make known and develop the image, or to acquire and/or retain customers and prospects – brands are first and foremost senders of messages. Each brand has a number of ways – the media – to implement its own marketing communication policy.

Action levers

Until relatively recently, the "mainstream media" or mass media, such as television or the press, saw themselves as relays for the brand message.

With the Internet, it is now possible to advertise on websites and thus "push" a message to a relatively large and qualified audience, in accordance with affinity with the target, thanks to the audience of media plan sites, and also to send a message personalized to a greater or lesser extent, by email or via an SMS, for example, to a set of prospects or customers.

Digital media, therefore, like traditional media, allow push marketing actions to be implemented but also – and this is what gives them their great specificity – to authorize the implementation of pull marketing actions, where the brand invites rather than, as push can too often give the impression, "imposes" its presence.

Think interactive

Inviting the audience to participate, making one's brand content always available, or getting Internet users to create or co-create their own brand experience are all opportunities that social media, such as Facebook, as well as brand sites, YouTube videos or blogs and forums make possible.

With the Internet and digital media, it is often said that communication, too often confined to a monologue, has finally acquired its full meaning. More than ever before, brands have a responsibility, even an obligation, to enter into dialog with their audiences. The most skilful brands at this level are, moreover, those that do best and are often some of the most respected and most popular, for example the Apple brand.

Better mixture means better communication

Instead of the policy of push that has long characterized marketing, digital marketing leaves room for a mix of push and pull. The brand must, of course, be widely disseminated, but must also (re)position itself at the level of its consumers, be open, available, ready to listen and share its content, and go beyond simply addressing people directly (through its policy of push). All this can be done by means of pull, for example through the word of mouth of its ambassadors and fans (on the Internet and beyond).[2] Digital marketing thus allows both push and pull to be fully used so that the brand can express itself and encourage feedback and dialog.

The idea of feedback is also central for measuring effectiveness, since it allows the concept of "response" to a marketing stimulus to be introduced. Indeed, we could represent the effectiveness of a marketing campaign simply by its capacity to achieve the goals that have been set. We develop this topic in more detail below.

The effectiveness of digital marketing

The issue of return on investment (ROI)

Effectiveness refers to the ability of a person, group or system to achieve its goals and objectives, or those that have been set for it. Being effective means producing the expected results and achieving the agreed objectives in a timely manner. Objectives can be defined in terms of quantity, quality, timeliness, costs, profitability, and so on. The concept of effectiveness is widely used in economics and management. Effectiveness should not be confused with efficiency, which characterizes the capacity to achieve objectives at the cost of an optimal consumption of resources – personnel, materials, finance. The term "effectiveness" is often associated with the concept of return on investment.

As marketing is an aspect of management science, it is not surprising to find the notion of effectiveness at the heart of the marketing process. "Marketing effectiveness" or ROMI (return on marketing investment) is one of the central concerns of marketing departments. The economic crisis of recent years has only amplified the phenomenon. The recent Ad Age CMO Strategy/Forrester CMO Group Survey, conducted among marketing departments of large US companies,[3] showed that, in 2011, chief marketing officers (CMOs) prioritized the maximization of return on marketing investments and not just the efficiency of these investments (we return to this topic later). In addition, marketing activities that are too expensive or too difficult to measure are quite simply dropped. These same US marketing managers made social media and digital marketing their number two priority for 2011.

In France, and in Europe more generally, the same priorities apply. As of November 2008, the effectiveness of marketing actions was the leading priority for CMOs. Our recent conversations with major industry associations confirm this trend. The same is true at a European level, as evidenced by the digital initiatives of advertisers through the World Federation of Advertisers (WFA) and digital industry experts through the Interactive Advertising Bureau (IAB) Europe.

Structural needs: necessary structural changes

In the case of France, the UDA e-marketing barometer is instructive, since it shows that even if the level of expertise of French advertisers in terms of knowledge and use of digital media is progressing, only 45% of them (compared to 40% in 2010) believe they have a good or very good knowledge of the tools available.

While these advertisers applaud digital marketing for its low cost, its relative simplicity of implementation, and its greater efficiency, they consider that the absence of a dedicated team in their organization (55% in 2011, 25% in 2010) and the lack of expertise and information about its effectiveness (44% in 2011, 45% in 2010) are the main obstacles to its development. In the space of a year, while investments have continued to grow and the lack of specialists and dedicated teams has become increasingly noticeable, the expertise in terms of efficiency has not improved.

If things do not move forward on this last point, the whole profession and digital marketing will suffer as a result, and its development will be that much slower. However, according to the sector's professionals (see the Ad Age CMO Strategy/Forrester survey cited above), one only has to measure the effectiveness of digital marketing to see that is inevitable and even central to the marketing processes. So what is it in reality?

How effective is digital marketing? Can its effectiveness be measured? Do brands and marketing departments feel they have sufficient expertise on the subject? We shall see below that it is in regard to these points that much progress still remains to be made.

What does it mean to measure effectiveness?

The word "measure" refers to the need to "seek to know, to determine a quantity by means of a measurement." The measurement is the quantity used as the basic unit for evaluation. Measuring marketing effectiveness thus means assessing its effects, that is, evaluating the anticipated results and achieving the set objectives. Whatever the objectives of digital marketing – increasing awareness, brand image, esteem, sales, loyalty or commitment – measuring consists of updating a measurement, metric or key performance indicator (KPI), so as to assess the expected impact of the various objectives. All this may seem obvious, but my experience as a practitioner shows that resources are often deployed without really identifying the priority objectives of the actions envisaged. Do they increase awareness? Enhance the brand image? Increase sales? Without objectives, it is hard to set up a monitoring stage, or measure the return or effectiveness, that will be able to make use of measurements and metrics geared to the objectives.

Choosing metrics and indicators

In the process, it is the objectives that should allow the most appropriate measures to be decided on and kept up to date. These measures must be chosen in advance, that is, before the launch of the marketing campaign and not afterwards, as is too often the case.

It is not uncommon for advertisers and agencies to update a series of inappropriate (in relation to the objectives) measures or KPIs during or at the end of a campaign. Pressed for time, or more often because the "monitoring" stage of the marketing actions is inadequately planned, the relative ease of access to the metrics most often available free of charge (via tracking tools that specify the number of impressions given, the number of visits/visitors, the number of clicks) has the effect of not allowing the potential impact of a campaign to be accurately measured.

All too often the measures used are not suitable for the purpose, and in no time the medium that is supposed to be the most measurable of all media gains a reputation for being unable to quantify the effects of its actions – a considerable shame at a time when it is essential to demonstrate the effectiveness of marketing so as to justify investment and additional resources.

A special discipline

It is vital, even before addressing the choice of the most appropriate metrics, to recognize the importance of monitoring in the marketing process. Without monitoring, there can be no measurement, and without measurement there can be no monitoring, and therefore no optimal management of resources – "you cannot manage what you cannot measure."

Monitoring and measurement are therefore primarily a discipline, or a state of mind, which must be integrated upstream of the marketing process, in the same way as other activities. Measuring involves the formulation of clear objectives (because otherwise it is difficult to measure them), which requires a common language between the project's various actors, and this in turn facilitates communication and the development of marketing actions. If we are not clear about these objectives, and are unable to communicate and measure them, then the various stakeholders, particularly the financial and general departments, may well question the value of digital marketing.

Validity and reliability of measurement

Validity and reliability are the two necessary conditions for ensuring the quality of the instruments used and therefore the results obtained.

Validity

Validity refers to the capacity of the measure to correctly quantify or represent the concept or construct being measured. In other words, if the measurement of effectiveness seeks, for example, to verify the impact on brand image, a valid measure must be able to correctly measure the potential impact of the online campaign on the brand image.

Purists and academic marketing researchers want to verify:

- The *internal validity* of the effectiveness study, that is, to show that changes in the response variable (in our example, the measurement of the brand image) are caused solely by changes in the independent or explanatory variable. The explanatory variable in this case is the online campaign.
- *External validity* represents the possibilities (and limitations) of the extrapolation of the results and conclusions of the effectiveness study to the whole area that was the subject of the investigation, or possibly to a wider area.[4]

The development of appropriate measures

In practice, brand managers generally have confidence in their providers of studies and measurements, which in principle should ensure the validity of the measuring instruments deployed. Too often, however, because the measures and metrics used are unsuited to the campaign objectives, it is unlikely that the measure is "valid," since from the outset it is ill-adapted to the objective.

The most common case is the measurement of the branding effectiveness of online campaigns, that is, the capacity of campaigns to raise awareness and enhance the image, which today is too often evaluated using metrics such as the percentage of clicks, with generally less than 0.5 percent of clicks on a campaign. It is impossible to estimate the branding effect, not because of the low click level, but simply because the measure itself is unsuitable for the purpose; it is therefore "invalid" (in the sense of its internal validity).

The results of a campaign test may be considered externally valid if the entire campaign has been correctly measured and if the other variables, which may influence these "monitored" outcomes, have been taken into account in measuring the overall effect of the campaign; for example, the presence and effect of the TV media plan in the case of a TV plus online campaign.

It is, however, difficult to extend and expand the results to all campaigns and brands of a product category, as the results are generally dependent on the context in which the campaign is conducted and therefore tested (media budget, competitors' media plans, and size of the brand).

Nevertheless, the experience accumulated by the companies specializing in measuring effectiveness, which take the form of sectoral "standards" and benchmarks, makes it possible to situate the results and provide guidance and lessons "about what works and what does not work," as well as optimization methods. Once the validity of the measure has been established, its reliability must be checked.

Reliability

The reliability of a measurement instrument refers to its capacity to reproduce the same result when the same phenomenon is measured several times with the same instrument. In turn, sensitivity refers to the capacity of the instrument to record relatively small variations in the phenomenon measured.

Web analytics

In practice, what can we say about the reliability of digital marketing measurements? Take the case of web analytics, which includes all measurement tools of audience and traffic on the Internet and is able to quantify a website's audience and traffic based on indicators such as the number of unique visitors, page views, visits, and the average duration of visits. But before long, web analytics had to face concerns about the reliability of its measures.

Indeed, the analysis of log files, on which the first statistical analyses were based, was quickly limited to "faithfully"[5] collecting the number of visits, visitors, and so on. Log files were not originally directly intended for this analytical use, and measuring traffic was therefore developed with marker technologies or tags. Placed on each page of the site being measured, tags can count visits, visitors, and so on. This led to improved reliability of the measurements collected.

Even today the comparison of measures from web analytics tools, and using the same tag technology, such as Google Analytics or At Internet solutions, often produces different measurements when they are installed on a given site.

Complementarity of metrics

Similarly, "site-centric" audience measurements – tools based on measurement using tags – and "user-centric" audience measurements – based on the observation of recruited panels (usually those of Nielsen Online, formerly known as Nielsen NetRatings, and comScore) and Internet user representatives, whose behavior is measured over time – are not comparable. The figures are often different and are largely fueled by heated exchanges between supporters of one or other of the measures. In reality, of course, these two measures are complementary.

But beyond this complementarity, the reality of the practice of measuring on the Internet shows that it is complex, difficult to implement, and often imperfect. Yet could we manage without it?

It is because matters are difficult that "discipline" is essential for understanding and controlling them better.

Measurement is above all a discipline, without which it is difficult to advance. Although some people have long asserted that the Internet is the most measurable of the media and therefore the one on which we can "measure everything," this is not the case. *On the web, we can unquestionably "count" (admittedly with varying degrees of reliability), but counting is not measuring.*

As we have already seen, measuring effectiveness means coming up with valid and reliable indicators, in line with the objectives targeted by the digital strategy. This process is difficult, and often imperfect. But can we dispense with this discipline? The answer is assuredly no.

It is often better to have tools that are imperfect but offer a more than 50 percent chance of making the right decision (clearly better than simply tossing a coin), rather than give free rein to intuition alone.

Digital marketing, like marketing in the broadest sense, is an art and a science. The science of measurement, however imperfect, enables decisions to be made more objectively and, in particular, enables management to understand, evaluate, and justify its investments. It is thus better to have approximate metrics, "proxy metrics" – even though one should always endeavor to refine and improve them – which admittedly do not always allow the most accurate measurement, but have the great merit of being able to anticipate general trends quickly rather than simply "flying by the seat of one's pants." At a time when the need for metrics and ROI are among companies' day-to-day concerns, such is the price for the legitimacy of digital marketing and the greater attention paid to it.

Measuring rather than simply counting

To clearly understand the ins and outs of the measurement of the effectiveness of digital marketing, it is essential to differentiate between these two concepts – measuring and counting.

Counting is what best describes the much-vaunted measurability of the web. The Internet was presented from the outset as the supreme medium, where everything could be measured and therefore evaluated and whose effectiveness could be truly ascertained. The celebrated "click" then seemed to be the best remedy against the need for evidence and measuring the impact of the first advertisers on the web. "Advertise on my website and the number of clicks will show you how many people have been in direct contact with your brand." An enticing prospect, since compared to the mass media that reach a huge audience but whose possible impact (following advertising exposure) is not directly measurable, the argument for advertising on the Internet is particularly persuasive. But before long, click-through rates quickly fell – for advertising that was novel initially is no longer so, and has even become intrusive, as banners are transformed into pop-ups, and then into interstitials, to increasingly force exposure – and are today well below 0.5 percent.

Even if Internet penetration is still growing and progressing, it is difficult to obtain an audience coverage as strong and instantaneous as that offered by television. Therefore, for websites and the profession in general, it was necessary to show as quickly as possible that on the Internet one could "measure more" and provide more indicators and metrics; and all of sudden, the Internet had become "the most measurable of all the media." In fact, it is easy to count everything, or almost everything (the number of visitors and visits, time spent, the number of impressions delivered by the campaign), but more difficult to measure an effect, especially when it is indirect. But despite this, the false truth that "on the Internet you can measure everything" quickly entered into advertising agencies' claims and promises of "results," and the reputation of the Internet was assured, or almost so. Yet, when one tries to demonstrate that "it works" and that it is "effective," especially for campaigns that do not have specific online sales targets and are not therefore directly measurable, it is much more difficult to measure the effects.

Since then, 15 years have passed. Internet penetration and accessibility are high, media consumption is increasingly fragmented, and young people born in the era of the Internet, generation Y, cannot manage without it. The Internet and, more recently, social networks accompany them everywhere through their mobile phones (cf. "SoLoMo" – social-local-mobile). Digital media are becoming indispensable, and brands are beginning to take them on board and increase their online investment. But as we have said, this progression will continue to grow only on condition that measuring rather than simply counting becomes the rule for all web actors.

Measuring means first and foremost establishing clear marketing objectives, identifying the most appropriate metrics, assessing the achievement of these objectives, and setting up the most pertinent measurement system (and not just "counting" on the basis of the sometimes appropriate, sometimes too limited metrics from web analytics); measuring, evaluating, and correcting in order to advance and increase the effectiveness of digital marketing. Measurement comes at a price, primarily that of discipline. But ROI is stronger for it, and it allows a "balancing of the books" at the end of the campaign for the benefit of all stakeholders – brands, agencies, media, and measurement providers.

Users of ROI measurement and their needs

It seems important to devote a few paragraphs to the key stakeholders in the measurement of effectiveness and, more generally, in digital marketing, because their profession, role, and position in the "digital marketing" value chain keep up-to-date expectations and sometimes assumptions, which are often different from the notion of "effectiveness monitoring." This prior understanding is essential for defining the basis of a common language and goals on which all parties need to be able to have a dialog in order to evaluate the performance of their marketing campaigns.

There are generally four types of actors in the digital marketing value chain: the advertiser, the advertising or "digital" agency, the media agency, and the measurement company (usually a research company). A fifth participant may sometimes be inserted between these actors, usually at the request of the advertiser, adviser or consultant, who may recommend an approach or process suitable for the establishment of objectives and therefore appropriate measures.

The advertiser

The advertiser is naturally the party who has the greatest interest in monitoring effectiveness. Indeed, brands invest in digital media (and other media) in order to build and maintain their presence and brand capital, whatever the objective targeted, for example branding, esteem, the acquisition of new customers, or developing the loyalty of existing customers.

As we have discussed above, the brand must make clear its objectives to the agency. The agency will then be responsible for developing and executing a plan (the copy strategy) to achieve them. The measurement of effectiveness should be directly related to the monitoring and attainment of these objectives. Such monitoring is essential, and should allow:

- the return on investment to be evaluated
- lessons to be drawn so as to further optimize the impact of actions
- past and future investment to be justified.

Realities in the field

The effectiveness monitoring stage would seem to be indispensable, but in fact this is far from being the case.

> A recent study[6] conducted in the USA with 252 companies, representing a marketing investment of more than $50 billion, shows that:
>
> - 61% of the companies do not have a defined and documented process allowing them to select, evaluate, and prioritize their various marketing campaigns.
> - 69% do not use a test/monitoring approach to monitor and evaluate the impact of their campaigns.
> - 73% do not have a scorecard allowing them to assign clear marketing/business objectives to their campaigns before financing them.

In short, these results suggest that the majority of companies have no process in place for managing and genuinely evaluating their marketing investments. For the most part, they do not incorporate metrics into the daily management of their marketing activities.

Conversely, companies that are leaders in their markets have established a more documented and quantified approach to the impact of their marketing investment. Such companies benefit from a real competitive advantage.[7] More specifically, Professor Tom Davenport, of Babson College, USA, has shown that these companies have a number of common characteristics:

- Management that supports and imposes quantitative management of investments. Analytics is central, since decisions are fact based.
- Simple descriptive statistics have given way to more analytical and predictive decision-making models.
- The use of analytics goes beyond the marketing function and is central to all business functions.
- Data analysis structures the organization and shapes its operation – "an enterprise-level approach to managing analytical tools."

My own consulting experience, in Europe and in the USA, confirms these conclusions. It is generally not so much digital marketing and its supposed measurability that dictates the advertiser's monitoring process but rather the culture of the company itself. Typically, the more the company is accustomed to metrics for managing, the more it will seek to incorporate the measurement of the effectiveness of digital marketing. A good example of this is provided by Procter & Gamble (P&G), the largest global advertiser.

Even though P&G's online investment is growing, it is not yet at the level of other companies. However, the company quickly became interested in measuring the performance of its digital investments. In the case of P&G, it is typically less the size of the investment and more the culture of measurement that dictates the need for monitoring.

Conversely, other companies less accustomed to measuring and managing their business by means of metrics have more difficulties, but they too have less and less choice.

As we have seen, with Internet investment increasing and the recent economic crisis having imposed greater rigor, it needs to be shown more than ever that marketing and digital initiatives are effective or at least "are heading in the right direction." Measurement is becoming not only more important but will soon be unavoidable. Much to the chagrin of some advertising agencies, certain advertisers have clearly grasped this and are beginning to question their agency's traditional compensation model.

Purchasing and marketing procurement departments are gradually switching from compensation generally based on fees and commissions to a model more focused on performance. Taking into account the ROI generated by campaigns is a basic tendency. There is certainly a shift toward a hybrid compensation model comprising fees, commissions, and a variable component linked to ROI.[8]

Agencies

Are effectiveness measurement and agency creativity compatible?

Within agencies, the question of effectiveness measurement is not new, nor is it confined to digital media. I remember my first years in the profession, in the early 1990s, when international advertisers were beginning to intensify the globalization of their marketing practices, and the standardization of advertising's effectiveness measurement already animated many debates. More than 20 years later, the world's leading advertisers have accepted the need to manage and measure the effectiveness of their advertising, particularly in the area of consumer goods.

Today, in the era of global campaigns, it is no longer possible not to pre-test, post-test and evaluate the effects by means of tools such as "ad tracking." Whether the creatives like it or not, no more campaigns without tests. Oscar Jamhouri,[9] president and founder of Integrated Marketing Communication, and himself a former adman, often says that it is difficult, or even impossible, to measure creativity in advertising, but, on the other hand, it is possible to measure its effects, and that's what matters. So what bearing does all this have on the Internet?

Paradoxically, as we have already discussed, digital marketing is often poorly evaluated, as the metrics are not necessarily always appropriate to the objectives and often not adequately assessed. Indeed, the rapid deployment and lower cost of digital marketing campaigns (compared to other media) too often lead to the effectiveness monitoring stage being neglected. This is sometimes considered too expensive (given the cost of the campaign itself). Yet, if monitoring is omitted, it is difficult to judge the effects of the campaign and therefore to justify the digital investment.

Whatever parts of the industry may think, the measurement of advertising effectiveness, including digital advertising, is becoming increasingly unavoidable. In fact, there is currently a fundamental trend in which the most prominent agencies are aiming to include more metrics in their service offering. There are two situations: some agencies are themselves incorporating studies and metrics in the consultancy provided, while others are teaming up with research companies to provide measurements of the effectiveness of their campaigns. It is difficult to be both judge and judged, and in our opinion, the market will soon organize itself, as has happened with measuring the impact of TV, with the emergence of independent specialists for measuring the effectiveness of digital marketing. In the USA, for example, Dynamic Logic, part of Millward Brown, a company historically positioned in this market, is experiencing rapid growth as online media investment accelerates.

Alain Heureux
President and CEO, IAB (Interactive Advertising Bureau)
Europe

Please tell us in a few words what IAB Europe is?

IAB Europe is the voice of digital business. Its mission is to protect, prove, promote, and professionalize Europe's online advertising, media, market research, and analytics industries. Together with its members – companies and national trade associations – IAB Europe represents over 5,500 organizations.

While digital media budgets continue to increase, what would you say are the main barriers for advertisers' continuous investment in digital marketing?

We've indeed reached the 25% average market share in 2012 for Europe but main hurdles remain the cross-media comparability as traditional and new media are still not aligned toward common measurement standards. Brand safety and legal risks must also be mentioned.

Are digital marketing ROI and effectiveness often discussed between members of IAB Europe? What initiatives are IAB Europe planning to further support the market around better "digital accountability?"

We've set up a new committee called the Brand Advertising Committee, grouping over 25 experts debating standardization, measurement, and monetization representing the entire ecosystem, which includes agencies, advertisers, and media aiming for the definition and deployment of metrics for brand advertising throughout Europe.

In general, everyone in the profession agrees on one point. The media need to be measured in order to be evaluated and thus enable brands to reach their audience. Thus, audience measurement is in a way the "currency of exchange" that allows the media market to structure itself. It was therefore natural that with the emergence of the Internet as a medium, audience measurement was a fundamental issue – for websites of course (that want to sell advertising space), but also for media agencies, which want to offer their clients (brands and advertising agencies) appropriate media planning.

The first major moves in audience measurement began in the mid-1990s, with the setting up of the leading player, the US company Media Metrix, which then established itself in Europe through partnerships with Ipsos and GFK. NetValue, a French company started with a fundraiser and then listed on the stock market with a market capitalization of more than €100 million, began offering its services in Europe. Media Metrix was acquired by comScore, while NetValue was bought by NetRatings, which was itself acquired in its entirety by Nielsen in 2007.

In little more than 10 years, the market for audience measurement had stabilized, although there is still an area of "uncertainty" about the accuracy of the measurements provided. User-centric and site-centric approaches are different but remain complementary, even if it is sometimes difficult to reconcile and compare audience numbers in absolute terms. Although this may seem unimportant, it is in fact fundamental, because if the medium's unit of measurement, its "currency of exchange," is not understood, accepted, and recognized, the entire digital ecosystem falters and cannot develop as it should.

Of course, there is no lack of initiatives to rationalize the system, for example ANA (Association of National Advertisers), the IAB, and the 4A's (American Association of Advertising Agencies),[10] and IAB Europe and WFA),[11] but it is not easy for all the parties to agree. As we have seen, measuring the Internet is difficult and will remain so, and at this stage, it is still not a matter of measuring effectiveness, but simply "counting" and evaluating the audience.

Despite these problems, media agencies remain, without a doubt, the link in the digital value chain that has contributed most to the development of Internet measurement, but primarily with a view to "enumerating" audiences, rather than the effectiveness of campaigns, together with a desire to legitimize the Internet and place it on a par with the other "mainstream media."

Research companies

We are concerned here more with the measurement of effects rather than the "enumeration" of audiences. This responsibility often falls within the competence of market research and advertising research companies. As investment grows, the measurement of effects also tends to increase.

The market for measuring the effectiveness of digital marketing began to take shape with the appearance of traditional actors in advertising effectiveness studies, such Ipsos ASI, Nielsen Online and Millward Brown, which, through the acquisition of specialized Internet players, attempted to expand their offerings or develop their own tools.

Other independent actors positioned in this sector from the outset, such as CRM Metrix and MetrixLab, both founded in 2000, have grown at a rate matching that of Internet investment. In all cases, the measurement of digital and its effects is a profession that simultaneously requires competence in conducting surveys, Internet technologies, and the specificities of digital marketing. Our discussions with the most advanced advertisers in this area confirm this: "being or becoming a specialist in measuring digital media takes time."

For example, whereas in the case of international TV campaigns, evaluation is almost always left to the traditional big players in market research, when it comes to digital, independent companies, smaller in size but specialized, are not only sought out, but often win the bids. In all cases, be they small or large, companies measuring the effectiveness of digital marketing will become essential because, as we have explained, the digital market and, in particular, its advertisers increasingly need measurements to justify the ROI of their investments.

E X P E R T   V I E W P O I N T

Steven Rappaport
Director of knowledge, the Advertising Research Foundation (ARF)

As the director of knowledge for the Advertising Research Foundation (ARF), you are in an ideal role to witness the evolution of media and marketing. How would you say that "digital" is reshaping the practice of marketing?

Digital has influenced advertising, but I do not think it has reshaped it yet. Three influences are evident: advertising on demand; advertising as a service; and advertising as engagement. Important as the emergence of these influences are, breakthrough digital advertising strategy is elusive because the industry appears hopelessly locked into conventional mass media thinking. Digital and social media were born from a communications protocol, TCP/IP, which was designed for people to communicate, share, and collaborate with one another. Advertisers and agencies never grasped that; they have spent precious time and resources to recreate the familiar mass media world within the digital one. While it is undeniable that a few brands are digitally brave, BMW is one, and others have exploited some digital capabilities such as augmented reality, it is also undeniable that most brands do not think digitally. If they did, they would be create a new type of advertising that takes its inspiration from TCP/IP and reshapes – and reimagines – advertising.

In the course of this book, we will try to provide various reference points, tools, and perspectives to enable all actors to better understand, manage, and optimize the effectiveness of their digital marketing. The core of our contribution is to define and explain the concepts, while putting into practice the use of metrics and quantitative or qualitative indicators to measure the effectiveness of digital marketing. The aim is to demystify the field, and thus allow all players, big and small, to develop a process, a discipline, and tools that will enable them to better ascertain the impact and ROI of their digital marketing.

Key points

1 Digital marketing is an evolved form of marketing, governed by a combination of push and pull.

2 The effectiveness of digital marketing is crucial for profitability and sustainability for all players and the whole digital ecosystem.

3 Measuring effectiveness goes beyond the simple "counting" that too often characterizes digital initiatives, and allows the attainment of the campaign's objectives to be verified.

Notes

1   Cova, B. (2008) "Consumer made: when the consumer becomes producer," *Decisions Marketing*, 50: 19–27.
2   Since 2007, the US marketing consultancy Keller Fay Group has been attempting to quantify the magnitude of "word-of-mouth marketing", and has shown that every year more than 80 percent of conversations about a brand occur offline rather than online – by telephone, face to face or among friends.
3   The Top Priorities of CMOs in 2011: Ad Age CMO Strategy/Forrester CMO Group Survey, see http://adage.com/article/cmo-strategy/budgets-innovation-squarely-cmos-sights-2011/148070/.
4   For more information on the concepts of reliability and validity, see Farris, P.W., Bendle, N.T., Pfeifer, P.E and Reibstein, D.J. (2010) *Marketing*

Metrics: The Definitive Guide to Measuring Marketing Performance (2nd edn) Prentice Hall.

5 In the specialist measurement literature, reliability and loyalty are synonymous.

6 See the study carried out by the Kellogg School of Management, in Jeffery, M. (2010) *Data-Driven Marketing: The 15 Metrics Everyone in Marketing Should Know*, Wiley, p. 4.

7 See the excellent book on the subject, Davenport, T.H. and Harris, J.G. (2009) *Competing on Analytics: The New Science of Winning*, Harvard Business School Press.

8 Dan, A. (2011) "Lack of measurement and innovation has turned agencies into 'vendors,'" January, http://adage.com/article/cmo-strategy/advertising-agencies-innovate-work-procurement/148491/.

9 www.integration-imc.com/oscarcv.htm.

10 The ANA (Association of National Advertisers), the IAB (Interactive Advertising Bureau), and the 4A's (American Association of Advertising Agencies) announced the release of the Guiding Principles of Digital Measurement in June 2011. These five principles are the foundation of *Making Measurement Make Sense*, an ecosystem-wide initiative independently facilitated by the management consulting firm Bain & Company and the strategic advisory firm MediaLink.

11 WFA (2009) "What advertisers want from online audience measurement," position paper, April, www.wfanet.org/pdf/med_documents/Whatadvertiserswantfromonlinemeasurement.pdf.

chapter 2

The digital market and the main objectives of digital marketing

Executive summary

- The digital market is growing fast and is expected to account for at least 20 percent of advertising expenditure by 2017. Through its various levers – search, display, affiliation, email, mobile, and social media – it allows brands to implement their complete marketing strategy, from the development of awareness and the image through to acquiring new customers or developing their loyalty.
- The brand's digital ecosystem is structured around its presence in paid media, owned media and earned media (POEM).
- The AIDA model (attention, interest, desire, action) allows the objectives assigned to a digital marketing strategy to be structured.

The digital market

The digital market should be understood in two ways. It is a market of media, some of which are pure players (originating with and built around the Internet), while others, such as press or TV, are in the process of being digitized. The latter media retain a number of traditional characteristics that constitute their DNA. The progressive digitization of these media calls into the question the conventional approaches to advertising effectiveness. Such approaches are subject to revision as new techniques for reaching consumers develop.

The digital market consists of several segments, each of which is an ecosystem in its own right. The relative importance of these segments and changes in the market are shown in Figure 2.1. Each domestic market differs in size and evolution, but across the board, search remains the leading segment of online interactive marketing and communications. Display advertising follows, with a developing trend toward more investment in both mobile advertising and social media specifically.

The search market

The search market consists of the purchase of keywords. These keywords are bought at auction from search engines and enable text ads to be constructed, which are seen under the "sponsored links" heading of results pages. In many countries, in 2011, Google had more than 80% share of the search market. Purchases are made through its Google Adwords program and also include a network of partners (websites, blogs, partner search engines), the so-called "display network."

Text ads benefit from rather favorable investment environment, for the following reasons:

1 The number of searches is growing globally:
   - 131 billion queries worldwide in 2011 (comScore)
   - up 46% compared to 2008
   - 29 million searches every minute.

   The leaders are the USA with 22 billion queries per year, China with 13.2 billion and Japan with 9 billion. France ranks sixth overall.

2 Text ads are becoming more effective, particularly through better use of investment feedback levers, such as the call to action buttons that encourage Internet users to click and the landing pages to which users are redirected after clicking.

Interactive marketing overall will near $77 billion by 2016

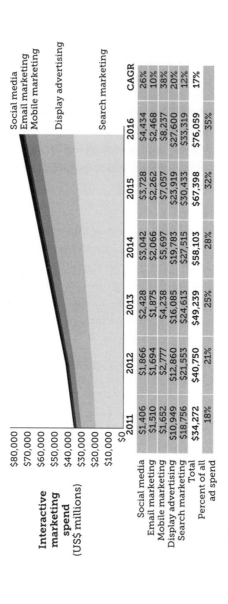

Interactive marketing spend (US$ millions)	2011	2012	2013	2014	2015	2016	CAGR
Social media	$1,406	$1,866	$2,428	$3,042	$3,728	$4,434	26%
Email marketing	$1,510	$1,694	$1,875	$2,066	$2,262	$2,468	10%
Mobile marketing	$1,652	$2,777	$4,238	$5,697	$7,057	$8,237	38%
Display advertising	$10,949	$12,860	$16,085	$19,783	$23,919	$27,600	20%
Search marketing	$18,756	$21,553	$24,613	$27,515	$30,433	$33,319	12%
Total	$34,272	$40,750	$49,239	$58,103	$67,398	$76,059	17%
Percent of all ad spend	18%	21%	25%	28%	32%	35%	

FIGURE 2.1 The various online communication channels and their evolution, 2011–16, USA

Source: Forrester's US Interactive Marketing Forecasts, 2011 to 2016.[1]

3 Mobile connections open up new development prospects for the search market. For example, in many developed and developing economies, people access the Internet via their mobile phones, and more than 70% carry out Internet searches through their phone. For example, in the USA, mobile search (sponsored links on mobile phones) accounts for between 16% and 22% of online ad spending.

4 Geolocated searches are growing rapidly.

The display market

The display market is the segment covering traditional advertising or branding. The relatively low click-through rate (CTR) recorded for this type of ad (0.09% in France and 0.07% in the USA) does not discourage the market's creativity and buoyancy. Two factors account for this vitality. First, purchase is increasingly made by auction. Real-time bidding (RTB) allows one's advertising to be seen based on the auctions one agrees to. These auctions focus on behavioral targeting (for example skiers) and are generally based on the cost per thousand impressions. For example, in 2012, RTB concerned nearly 10% of online shopping in France, against more than 20% in the USA. Second, the creativity of formats is an important factor in the dynamics of the market. The use of these formats varies according to their capacity to create interaction with Internet users. Video is booming and is driving growth in the market, since advertisers are constantly looking for interactivity and greater audience commitment.

The email market

Emailing is the most threatened market segment, but is also the segment that has historically been the most "effective" for "tracking" consumer behavior. The relative stability of expenditure on it in recent years (compared to other segments, all of which are growing) illustrates the crisis it faces. In fact, emailing needs to adapt to marketing management objectives:

1 Homogenize the company's overall communication.

2 Strengthen proximity between the customer and the brand.

3 Be consistent across all channels.

4 Communicate in a personal and relevant way with every customer.

5 Increase the ROI of marketing actions.

These objectives seems perfectly suited to emailing. Nevertheless, a revolution in usage and congestion of the emailing market is threatening it. Email is less used by the 15–24 age group, with social networks being more popular and viewed as less "spammed."[2] Email offers CTRs and opening rates that vary considerably according to the sector.

The affiliation market

Figure 2.2 shows how the affiliation market is structured.

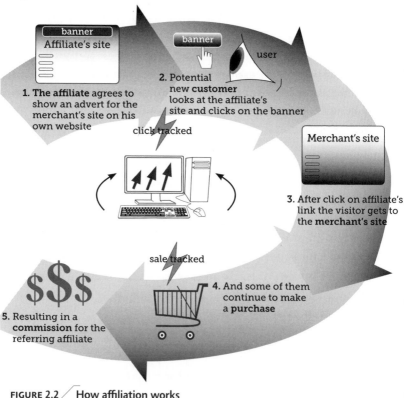

FIGURE 2.2 How affiliation works

Affiliation allows any website or blog having an advertising space to be monetized. As with display, an intermediary is inserted between the affiliator who wants to advertise and the affiliate who wants to sell his space. Denoix summarizes the principles of affiliation in Table 2.1.

TABLE 2.1 Principles of affiliation

	Affiliation contract
Contracting parties	Affiliator and affiliate
Nature of relationship	Partnership
The Internet user's actions generate remuneration	Single visit to the affiliator's website (payment by click or cost per click) Completing a form (payment by lead or cost per lead) Making a purchase (payment by purchase, fixed amount or commission)
Type of advertising message	Text links, banners, emails (affiliator's databases)
Duration of contract	Indefinite and can be terminated at any time by either party

Source: Adapted from Denoix (2010).[3]

Denoix[3] distinguishes nine types of affiliate, ranging from emailers (who send emails for the affiliator), blogs and price comparers through to keyworders (who buy keywords on behalf of the affiliator).

The affiliator's campaigns should be as attractive as possible for the affiliates. The success of the campaign depends on their attractiveness, which is based on the creations providing content or the incentivizing remuneration system. Two relatively simple indicators here are:

• Is my campaign arousing interest? How many affiliates want to relay it?
• Are these affiliates likely to bring me leads?

Estimating an affiliation campaign's performance is therefore based on its capacity to retain and generate loyalty in the top affiliates, that is, those affiliates who bring in the largest number of qualified contacts or the most sales. The inventiveness of compensation systems follows the complexity of navigation by Internet users and the increasingly criticized last click rule, which says that the last site the user has clicked before conversion should be remunerated. Thus, remuneration methods oscillate between payment for performance (sales, leads brought in) based on a percentage of the sales figure and a simple cost per click, or even a combination of the two. However, the low figure per click or lead (around 0.25 cents) has made affiliation a good lever for price comparing big market players. The best affiliates are rarely blogs or websites with little traffic, unless the campaign has a purely qualitative axis.

The booming mobile market

Mobile telephony genuinely constitutes a fifth medium in the market. Like the Internet, it is a medium that embodies all the others – TV, radio, augmented reality display, Internet, cinema – with the major characteristics of mobility and its corollary, geolocation.

In addition, the mobile phone is:

- The first medium that is always handheld (making it an intimate tool).
- The first medium that is mostly – or perhaps always – switched on, making the consumer reachable at all times.
- The first medium that is also a means of payment, thus allowing the world of advertising and the world of purchase to be brought together as effectively as the Internet.
- The most effective medium for developing user-generated content, since consumers have the same device for creating photos and videos and sharing them with their friends or social networks.
- The best medium for tracking consumers: tracking their navigation on the Internet, their purchases, their consumption habits through geolocation, their age and gender, and even their virality potential, since Internet service providers know the incoming numbers and outgoing numbers.
- Probably the most "measurable" of media.

In 2007, the market for mobile advertising in the USA was worth $320 million, and in 2013 it is expected to reach $1.5 billion, or 112 percent growth. According to the weekly magazine *Stratégies*, the market in France stood at €23 million in 2009, with 10–15 million people connecting to the Internet by mobile phone. Mobile market dynamics vary largely by geography depending on mobile phone usage and digital marketing investment in general. However, many experts claim it will be the advertising market of the future, a prediction that needs to be supported by facts, as although relative growth is important, absolute investments remain modest compared to other online communication channels. Almost 1 million applications are available on the market.

In Chapter 1 we briefly defined digital marketing. This step seemed to us to be important to enable the reader to better understand the different communication channels that are available in digital advertising. We can now review the main objectives of digital marketing and marketing in general.

The main objectives of digital marketing

Publicizing one's brand has always been one of the primary concerns of marketing. Awareness, which can be defined as "the ability of a potential customer to recognize and remember that a brand exists and belongs to a given product category," is the foundation of any communication strategy. The existence of a brand recognized by the consumer implies closeness, trust, and the desire to buy it. Awareness is the first essential stage in building a brand image rooted in a sector, a strong presence in the consumer's mind, and a significant capture potential for new targets and new geographical zones.

Awareness has enabled brand categories to be defined in accordance with the type of awareness concerned. Thus, top-of-mind awareness – being mentioned first by consumers – is confined to hegemonic brands, or the awareness associated with second rank brands that drive a market without being a leader. Creating attention, a preliminary to all awareness, becomes indispensable and leads to the development of creative levers prior to any persuasion. Within this attention paradigm, the notion of gross rating points (GRP) has acquired particular importance and structured the entire market.

Is awareness a "neglected" indicator in the digital age?

Building brand awareness involves a constant search for creativity, in order to capture the consumer's attention. Yet a variety of social changes suggest that advertising based solely on the creation of awareness is becoming less effective. Riou[4] identifies two traditional advertising mechanisms that no longer work today, causing brands to constantly extend the boundaries of creativity:

- *Conviction-persuasion:* my product is the best and I prove it by presenting a series of factual arguments.
- *Projection-identification:* the product is used by people we would like to resemble.

Doing the opposite to traditional models results in breaking new ground in terms of advertising effectiveness, reflecting major social changes:

1 Increasing fragmentation of Western societies into networks or tribes, which require advertisers and agencies to target their consumers ever more precisely.
2 The public's extensive knowledge of advertising and media, which legitimates campaigns based on the second degree and connivance.
3 Standardization of markets, some of which are struggling to innovate and can only differentiate themselves through advertising.
4 Considerable advertising overload, which drives some brands to systematically search for creations with high impact value.
5 Competition between agencies, which are too often evaluated in terms of the awards and prizes obtained for ads they created.

Brand awareness has become something that "goes with saying." Taking into account more sophisticated indicators (image items, satisfaction barometer, loyalty development) complicates the advertiser–agency relationship and the processes of assessing the effectiveness of advertising campaigns. At the same time, applying GRP to the Internet gives rise to controversy and debate. Finally, the attention paradigm is giving way to the digital paradigm of acquiring leads, while the notion of customer acquisition is slowly but surely being replaced by loyalty development, which is deemed more economical and effective for marketing budgets.

The end of acquisition or the advantage of loyalty development

This broad strategic and operational movement toward loyalty encompasses concepts such as customer orientation, one-to-one marketing and customer relationship management. It is supported by market saturation and the need to re-engage with customers in order to better take into account their needs and expectations. Consequently, performance indicators are changing as new segmentation data (for example recent segmentation, frequency, amount) and new indicators such as churn (percentage of customers lost) are taken into account.

Acquisition only is considered too expensive. This observation was first made in the 1980s and popularized by many authors, including Michael Porter,[5] who views loyalty as a barrier to entry, and Frederick Reichfeld,[6] who showed that a 5% increase in loyalty rates increased the value of an average customer from 25% to 100%. In addition, marketing measurements are developing as markets and customer approaches become more complex.

Finally, branding, which covers brand identity in the broadest sense, imposes its own effectiveness standards, based on memory, the increase in image items, and recognition. However, these indicators are developed as a counterweight to sales-based indicators, which are, of course, too restrictive with regard to the diversity of campaign objectives. We will return to this point in more detail when we discuss indicators that are truly adapted to the objectives assigned to digital campaigns, and more generally to digital marketing.

TABLE 2.2 Overview of marketing measurements designed to evaluate the results of marketing actions

Measurement	Percent of user companies	Percent that give the best score for evaluation of marketing performance
Awareness	78	28
Market share	78	36.5
Relative price	70	37.5
Number of complaints	69	45
Customer satisfaction	68	46.5
Distribution/availability	66	18
Total number of customers	65.5	40
Perceived quality/appreciation	64	35.5
Loyalty/retention	64	67
Perceived relative quality	62.5	61.6

Source: Originally from *Marketing and the Bottom Line* (2000), Tim Ambler, Pearson Education Limited. Author saw it in: Shaw, R. and Merrick, D. (2005) *Marketing Payback*, Financial Times/ Prentice Hall.[7]

The difficult emergence of digital gross rating point

GRP faces a number of limitations that undermine its legitimacy and make industry professionals envisage other, more relevant audience measurements. Having first emerged with the supremacy of television, GRP is now at a turning point in its history, forced to take into account the characteristics of the market's new dominant medium, the Internet.

The emergence of "digital GRP" is made difficult by the very structure of the Internet as a medium. While traditional media still operate on the basis of GRP, digital media have "forgotten" this measure, which has been swept aside by CPM (cost per thousand impressions), CTR, cost per lead, and so on. (Remember the supposed "supreme measurability" of the Internet as a medium.)

Yet digital GRP is having difficulty establishing itself as a practice, even though the Internet Advertising Bureau provides a consistent operational definition of Internet GRP.

The definition of GRP (gross rating point) for the Internet

GRP is the performance indicator of a media plan on a defined target. It is the average number of contact opportunities in an advertising campaign per 100 people targeted, and is equal to the sum of the audiences (as a percentage) for each insertion of the message.

So, if a website reaches 37.5 percent of men aged between 25 and 35 and if this target population has the opportunity to see the advertising message three times, the GRP is equal to 37.5 x 3 = 112.5. This notion of GRP can be adapted to the Internet, by taking account of the specificities of the medium. The opportunity to see is defined as an impression with advertising. Internet GRP is the number of opportunities to see generated by an advertising insert per 100 individuals of the target.

The nonadoption of GRP by digital market actors is a hindrance to its development. Indeed, GRP is an ROI indicator understood by all actors. It provides comparisons of campaign histories, a long-term view of advertising space purchase costs, and, to a lesser extent, allows multimedia plans (press, TV, posters) to be built, based on the same standard.

Unfortunately, the digital market remains outside these innovations, unless its own indicators overtake the rest of the market. This is a credible scenario, since the growing digitization of the press, television, radio, and posters will de facto lead to the gradual phasing out of traditional GRP.

The emergence of new brands and new competitive environments is leading to the marginalization of awareness in the communication process. Yet these new brands and new environments have never "worked on" their GRP performance. They give a new look to the digital market and its ROI. To illustrate these points, we consider a brand whose digital activities are relatively recent.

The Make Up For Ever brand

Make Up For Ever, a make-up brand for professionals, entered the B-to-C market with the ambition of becoming known to the general public. The awareness that Make Up For Ever is building is based on digital levers, with in-store advertising and the press also being used. The brand's aim is to transfer its professional make-up brand equity to the general public. The qualities of perfection, good appearance, and product superiority are within the reach of all. This new positioning is reflected in use of the Internet to get close to its target. The awareness built is based on transparency and closeness, even though the image is high end and conveys the upmarket features of the brand.

The HD Not Retouched campaign

The campaign depicts perfectly made-up young female models taking photos of themselves with their mobile phones. A so-called "immersive application" is created, allowing the consumer to zoom in on parts of the faces likely to have been retouched. The lack of any retouching is demonstrated each time. The interactive video is supplemented by repeat showings on the Internet of a web series enabling the consumer to find out about the casting and to choose new models for the brand. Experts in reality TV introduce viewers to the shoot, the jury's verdicts, and so on. The target that Make Up For Ever hopes to reach with this web series is in the 20–40 age range. The brand's absence on social networks has quickly been made good. Its Facebook page has more than 300,000 fans, and local pages (in Indonesia, Egypt, and so on) are being created.

Source: IAB.

This brand strategy follows an AIDA (attention, interest, desire, action) operating model, where, in "the economy of attention" that characterizes our society, awareness logically becomes the primary workhorse of brands, which have to exist and distinguish themselves within the mass of messages consumers are bombarded with. Push alone has to give way to push and pull feedback, where the brand has to organize its messages around the needs and desires of its customers and prospects. As we will see in Chapter 7, 360° communication has been succeeded by an integrated marketing communication model, in which the brand seeks to truly orchestrate its communication around the customer, alternating contacts in digital and offline (paid) media, its own contact points in owned media (brand sites, Facebook page, stores) and its earned media (that is, its capacity to induce word of mouth). We often say that the brand must exist and live in its own *communication ecosystem*. By ecosystem, we mean all the communications it can have with different publics through different points of contact. Before the Internet, such communication was largely vertical. Today, it is becoming

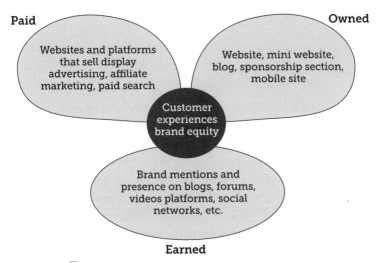

FIGURE 2.3 / POEM: paid, owned, earned media

increasingly horizontal. In terms of measurement, the consequences are simple enough: the brand must take into account the effects of the actions that it controls (online campaigns, TV and press, through its paid and owned media contact points) and others that it controls less or not at all (social networks and buzz that are part of earned media). In place of copy strategy alone, centered on messages in the various paid media, there is now a communication ecosystem in which the brand orchestrates the dissemination of its *brand content* by "writing" and deploying its "POEM," that is, paid, owned and earned media (Figure 2.3).

ROI from attracting the consumer's attention: the resurrection of the AIDA model

AIDA is an old advertising persuasion model, dating back to 1898. It is based on the idea that advertising persuades consumers in different stages. Each stage allows the individual to "come closer" to the brand, to the point where it is purchased or repeat purchased. The four stages of the AIDA model are:

Stage 1: attracting attention
Stage 2: arousing interest
Stage 3: inducing desire
Stage 4: causing action.

The logic of the AIDA model is based on the theory of advertising effects. However, it was more or less abandoned by researchers in favor of more sophisticated advertising persuasion models. The inclusion of variables such as attitude toward the brand, especially in the 1990s, went hand in hand with the rise of these new models. The AIDA model gradually underwent a series of changes. It became AIDAS (where S stands for consumer satisfaction) or AIDAC (C for conviction). The difficult operationalization of attention certainly caused its share of disaffection. However, AIDA is now back in favor, supported by the world of the Internet, including Google (see Figure 2.4), which "justifies" its AdWords advertising program on the ability of search advertising to step by step raise attention toward the sponsored link, develop interest, trigger desire, and drive action (eventually directly buying from the sponsored linked). Indeed, the current plethora of advertising renews the importance of being able to distinguish one's brand and arouse the consumer's curiosity. The contextual nature of ads on the Internet gives a new legitimacy to advertising effectiveness and targeting.

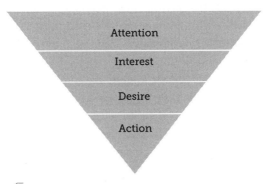

FIGURE 2.4 / The AIDA model

However, attracting consumers' attention is not enough to ensure the success of a campaign. Ongoing evaluation is the great strength of the web. But there are concerns about the poor performance of the CTR, which is in decline. Over two years, the number of users clicking on a banner has fallen from 32% to 16%, and today the average CTR lies between 0.06% and 0.15%.

One may wonder therefore about the real significance of this indicator. Advertising is not necessarily carried out to trigger an immediate purchase. Other persuasion mechanisms may come into play: familiarity with the brand, attribution, purchase intention, brand image on some items, and so on. These call for other indicators of effectiveness directly related to the different stages of the AIDA model.

More generally, this decline in the CTR indicates the need to reform measurement models on the Internet. However, the figures among different sources of web analytics do not match. What type of web analytics indicators purport to show the full spectrum of the possible impact of digital marketing? The web's "measurers" and "counters" that we described earlier need to redesign their organizations and their tools. "Social presence," an indicator that is totally absent from traditional advertising effectiveness measures, is a good example of a missing measurement of digital marketing ROI.

Thus the search for the "perfect" ROI necessarily means entering the maze that advertising has become: multiple contact points, positionings perceived differently by consumers than those wanted by brands, conversations on the web that cannot be controlled, extreme virality, and so on. But also, and particularly through the alignment of KPI metrics with realistic, shared, clear marketing objectives, *it is very much objectives that should guide the KPIs and not the availability of the many metrics* (usually relatively easily available on the web) that "produce the ROI."

E X P E R T   V I E W P O I N T

Pete Fader
Marketing professor, Wharton Business School

Did digital really change the way we need to do marketing? Is it easier or more difficult nowadays to drive effective marketing?

Of course, the digital era has meant massive changes to the practice of marketing. Some are obviously good, for example great ability to measure, tack, target, test, and so on. But some are bad, for example the lack of genuine thought that goes into marketing measurement today. We have really lost something from the old days, when the arrival of data was much slower, which forced managers/analysts to really think about the underlying factors driving the observed data they received. They were encouraged to make forecasts about what the next chunk of data would look like, and to spend some quality time looking at previous forecasts to continually refine their mental model of the data-generating process. Those days are long gone, never to be seen again, and a lot of the deep insights that arose from that process are making managers/analysts less capable of doing their jobs – despite the availability of better data.

So there are plenty of good things to celebrate and to take advantage of, but it's important to realize what we've lost in the process as well.

Coming back to "digital marketing ROI," what challenges and opportunities does it offer to brands?

A huge challenge and opportunity arises in the reframing of this question: instead of asking about ROI as it relates to particular brands, in many cases we should be asking about the ROI of particular customers. In the old days (and still today for many companies), we obsessed over the brand because it stood as a symbol of the relationship with our customers. Each customer was impossible to identify, measure, and target, so we built the brand under the assumption that a strong brand implies strong customer relationships. This notion may still be true today, but it is no longer necessary to rely exclusively on it. Virtually every marketer today can see themselves as a direct marketer, and they no longer need to rely on proxies for customer relationships. Thus, it may be more profitable for firms to focus on maximizing ROI through customer lifetime value (and/or other customer-centric measures) instead of product-centric measures. In no way does this diminish the importance of having a strong brand, but the power of the brand can be measured through customers, instead of the other way around.

In Chapter 3, we will review and explain the main metrics and KPIs available, and organize them in terms of digital marketing objectives, such as AIDA objectives, that can articulate them.

Key points

1. The digital market is composed of different segments, namely search, display, emailing, affiliation, mobile and social media.

2. The objectives of digital marketing are varied and complementary. Simply, the acquisition of new customers often associated with digital is giving way to more general brand development strategies involving awareness, the image, and loyalty. Each of the stages of the AIDA model (attention, interest, desire, action) can be activated through digital marketing.

3. The brand should be situated within its digital ecosystem and construct its "POEM" by deploying its paid, owned and earned media strategy.

Notes

1 VanBoskirk, S., with Spivey Overby, C. and Takvorian, S. (2011) US Interactive Marketing Forecasts, 2011 to 2016, Forrester, http://www.forrester.com/US+Interactive+Marketing+Forecast+2011+To+2016/fulltext/-/E-RES59379?docid=59379.

2 Spam or junk mail is the term for unsolicited and unwanted emails.

3 Denoix, A. (2010) *Affiliation: Build, Manage and Achieve an Effective Program*, Dunod.

4 Riou, N. (2002) *Marketing Anatomy: New Marketing Trends Scanned*, Eyrolles Editions.

5 Porter, M.E. (1996) "What is strategy?," *Harvard Business Review*, 74(6): 61–78.

6 Reichheld, F.F. with Teal, T.A. (2001) *The Loyalty Effect: The Hidden Force Behind Growth, Profits, and Lasting Value*, Harvard Business Press Books.

7 Ambler, T. (2000) "Marketing metrics," *Business Strategy Review*, 11(2): 59–66 in Shaw, R. and Merrick, D. (2005) *Marketing Payback*, Financial Times/Prentice Hall.

part 2

From the design to the implementation of a digital marketing effectiveness measure

Without returning to the differences and similarities between "counting" and "measuring," it is important to comprehensively review the various types of metrics and indicators available. After identifying and explaining these, we will try to situate them in relation to the objective of measuring digital marketing campaigns. We will then be able to provide a list of indicators for measuring the effects of specific digital actions.

The different types of metrics and KPIs available: "quantitative" vs. "qualitative"

Executive summary

- Measuring without an analytic framework is a pointless exercise: the AIDA model allows the objectives targeted by digital marketing and its effectiveness to be articulated.

- Although heterogeneous in terms of their definitions and measurement systems, "quantitative" and "qualitative" metrics can be used and combined to define key performance indicators (KPIs) for each point of contact (paid, owned, earned) and each stage of the AIDA model.

- Web analytics, advertising metrics, and consumer metrics are three types of metrics to be combined for a performing and operational digital marketing measurement system.

The different types of metrics

All the participants in the digital market generally seem to distinguish between "quantitative" and "qualitative" metrics. Intuitively, quantitative refers to "quantity," and thus to the capacity to measure, or take into account "mass effects," while qualitative metrics are for measuring, in more qualitative manner, the direct and indirect effects of exposure to a message.

They seek to better understand the profile of the individual thus exposed, their expectations, the quality of the interactive experience that exposure to the message provides, and the perceptions generated by the message.

With quantitative metrics, one typically seeks to measure the total audience of a campaign, the number of people who have actually been exposed to an advertising message, the number of times they saw it, or, for example, the number of clicks that the campaign generated. It is then a matter of "accounting" for the means deployed and the "directly quantifiable" – and often also easily quantifiable – effects: the number of clicks generated and the number of products sold on an e-commerce website, all of which comes back to the supposed high measurability of the Internet. In the strict sense of the term, accounting for refers to the notion of counting rather than measurement, concepts discussed and explained at length in Chapter 1. We will therefore assign to quantitative metrics the objective of counting the measures implemented by digital action as well as the objective of directly measuring the effects of a digital campaign.

As already mentioned, with qualitative metrics, one generally seeks to better understand the receiver and their understanding of the message and its effects. Did the person understand, and like, the message? Did the message induce changes in perceptions regarding the brand advertised? Qualitative metrics are especially useful when trying to better understand and measure the *potential* effects of a message, especially when it is difficult to determine and measure the direct and immediate effect of Internet exposure.

The case of the Omo washing powder brand

Like all consumer brands, Omo has a brand website (www.omo.fr), which highlights products, provides tips, and invites the visitor to find out more about the brand and its products. However, it is not possible to buy products directly from the website – although some promo codes can be downloaded – and it is difficult for the brand manager to truly estimate the impact of the site. The few traditional quantitative metrics

49

The different types of metrics and KPIs available: "quantitative" vs. "qualitative"

generally available, such as the number of unique monthly visitors or average time spent on the site, may be of value for ascertaining the site's audience level. But with only a few thousand visitors a month, it is difficult for the Omo brand manager to measure and enhance the effectiveness of the brand website. Indeed, how can the value of a few thousand visitors to the site be defended, when, for example, a prime-time TV advertisement will have an audience of millions of viewers, and where, in principle, it is certain to "hit" the target, the famous under-50 household? The same applies to Facebook pages, for which the vast majority of brands are far from having Coca-Cola's 35 million plus fans around the globe. Yet, should the number of fans be the sole criterion of success? What is the effect of exposure to brand websites or Facebook fan pages? Does exposure to them allow brand perceptions to be favorably changed? Such questions can be answered by means of qualitative metrics, with a view to enhancing and better defining the role and importance of each of these digital points of contact with the brand.

We will assign to qualitative metrics, therefore, the objective of enhancing the impact of the methods used by a digital campaign, as well as the objective of the generally intermediate measurement (change of perception of brand image, for example) and sometimes indirect measurement of the effects of digital exposure (as already mentioned, the brand website does not, in most cases, allow purchasing directly, but can, for example, encourage in-store purchase). We will go into greater detail later on these points by means of examples.

Adapting and choosing the most appropriate metrics and KPIs

As well as the specifics of both kinds of metrics – quantitative and qualitative – it is essential to update, adapt, and select the most suitable metrics for measuring each stage of the AIDA model. It is therefore the marketing objectives that should determine the choice of appropriate measurement indicators or KPIs. For example, *attracting attention*, the first stage of the AIDA model, can be measured (depending on the digital point of contact: website, Internet advertising, Facebook page) through quantitative and/or qualitative metrics. The number of visitors to a website may well be a measure of attention, just as memory or brand awareness following exposure to an ad or a digital campaign can serve the same purpose. Similarly, the second stage of the AIDA model, which concerns the *interest* aroused, can be measured by the click-through rate (CTR), an established and popular quantitative metric. Yet the CTR alone is unable to completely measure the full potential of exposure to a display banner campaign. For example, the memory generated and the interest aroused regarding the brand are important and necessary qualitative metrics for better measuring the impact of a campaign. It is therefore the alignment of metrics and measures to the objectives, and not the reverse, that is the key to success. Without this process of adjusting, from the outset, the implementation of the digital marketing plan, it is difficult to impartially assess and enhance the impact of its effects, and therefore the effectiveness of digital marketing. This same discipline should determine the implementation of digital marketing performance indicators, so as to bring up to date the KPIs capable of fully attaining, managing, and enhancing the impact of the implemented plan's objectives. Before going into the details of the various quantitative and qualitative measures available, it is important to discuss some essential principles for the establishment of KPIs.

Some essential principles for establishing the relevant KPIs

Key performance indicators, generally known as KPIs, are indicators for measuring how well a company performs. Their implementation and monitoring through performance or management dashboards are essential tools for decision-making and managing the present and future success of the business. Applied to the monitoring and control of the digi-

51

The different types of metrics and KPIs available: "quantitative" vs. "qualitative"

tal marketing plan, KPIs enable the ROI of its activities to be measured, developed, followed up, and optimized. In other words, KPIs become and are real tools for progress. Indeed – and this is essential – there is no point measuring something if it cannot be altered, improved, and optimized. It is here that the key issue of digital marketing lies. Everyone is getting involved in it and everything is being digitized, but what if you can't show that it works? Simple, one may say, but nonetheless essential. Without measurement, there is no management. And, in any case, you can only properly manage what you can measure.

Here, then, are 10 characteristics that make a measure a "good" indicator of performance:[1]

1 *It must be aligned with the objective of the digital plan, which is itself consistent with the brand/business strategy:* The objectives clearly determine the type and nature of the measures used. As we saw in Chapter 2, the measures must be valid and reliable: able to consistently measure changes attributable to digital marketing, they are in phase with the culture and strategy of the company and enable accurate tracking of performance over time.

2 *An individual or team has overall responsibility for it:* It is well known that without a boss, without someone in charge, it difficult to assign responsibilities and ultimately it becomes the responsibility of everyone and no one. What about companies that make their agencies responsible for measurement? Does this mean that measuring one's own performance is a matter only for a third party? Even if delegating the process of establishing KPI definitions saves time, sooner or later (indeed, sooner rather than later) everything must be reintegrated into the company and a champion appointed, a metrics boss, or at the very least a more or less systematic discipline must be imposed for monitoring the performance of digital marketing.

3 *It must allow action:* Able to follow the progress of operations implemented, the measures allow benchmarking, progress evaluation, and making adjustments if necessary – in short, enabling the company to be more efficient.

4 *It must allow forecasting:* KPIs reflect the intrinsic value of digital actions (everything comes back to the concept of "validity of measures"). The measures used should be able to take account of progress as well as any problems encountered by the digital marketing plan, so as to be able to anticipate and implement the necessary corrective actions.

5 *Limited in number:* It is well known that too much information kills information. It is therefore important to limit the number of KPIs. They should be both consistent with the objectives and aligned with the company's strategy and culture.

6 *They must be easy to understand and communicate:* Shared with and by everyone, the measures should be understood and appropriated by all interested parties, and should be clearly communicable, both internally and externally.

7 *They must be standardized:* Once defined and approved, they become the basis of a common language that is consistently applied and understood by all stakeholders: client/advertiser, media agencies, advertising agencies and market research companies.

8 *They must be "contextualized":* Measuring is fine, but knowing whether it is good, average or inadequate is even better. Without a context, it is difficult to progress and set realistic objectives. It is within this perspective that normative measures are necessary, since in return they allow ambitious, realistic objectives to be set and evaluated.

9 *They should be able to trigger change:* Measuring is a matter of understanding the past and present, but it is also projecting oneself into the future so as to steadily advance. Measurement is a discipline, and its systematic use is a source of progress.

10 *Keep them simple without being simplistic:* Measures should be easy to understand and communicate by virtue of being simple, but not "simplistic." It is in this latter respect that we can sometimes reproach the famous CTR, which, when misused or misinterpreted, can distort the effects of a digital action plan.

The different types of metrics and KPIs available: "quantitative" vs. "qualitative"

53

Georges Édouard Dias
Chief digital officer, L'Oréal Group

The year 2011 was the year of digital at L'Oréal. Can you tell us more?

With digital, consumers, our customers, go faster than the company itself. At the risk of being overtaken, we needed to send a strong signal from above and stick closer to the "pace" and requirements of our customers. So 2011 was the year of digital at L'Oréal, as the coming years will continue to be too. Digital is the responsibility of everyone in the company, not just the concern of a small group of specialists. From top management through to all the operational people, everyone is concerned.

How do the L'Oréal Group brands integrate digital into their marketing?

"Very naturally," because our business is "social" in nature. Beauty is a social phenomenon. Digital is therefore a real opportunity, because it allows us to provide feedback to the consumer. We should really be moving from "marketing by the book" to "marketing by the people." For our brands, this means:

- Understanding the "fingerprint" of each brand.
- Nourishing the conversation with the consumers of each brand.
- Using the richness of these insights to drive change and therefore one's marketing actions.

What procedures and initiatives are in place for assessing the contribution and ROI of digital marketing at L'Oréal?

We've fundamentally reviewed our "marketing model" approach, by centering more than ever around consumers and their buying cycle (in four stages). For each of the four stages of the buying cycle, we measure our performance using two KPIs:

- Consideration stage – KPI: *share of voice* and *top of mind*
- Evaluation stage – KPI: *share of search* and *purchase intent*
- Purchase stage – KPI: *share of market* and *conversion*
- Advocacy stage – KPI: *share of buzz* and *net sentiment.*

Overall success is measured by two global performance KPIs: *net promoter score*[2] and *sell out growth*.

As well as distinguishing the measures available in terms of their qualitative or quantitative character, it is important to distinguish them according to their origin and the type of use they can be put to. The aim here is to familiarize the reader with the main metrics available and their potential uses.

Metrics and KPIs derived from web analytics

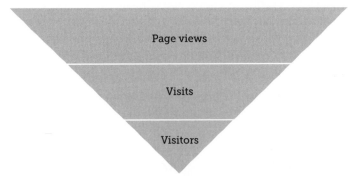

FIGURE 3.1 / The three metrics derived from web analytics

As a reminder, web analytics brings together all the tools for measuring audience figures and Internet traffic, which allow a website's audience and visits to be quantified on the basis of indicators. Web analytics metrics are

55

The different types of metrics and KPIs available: "quantitative" vs. "qualitative"

overwhelmingly "quantitative." For a complete overview of web analytics, we advise the reader to refer to the excellent book by our industry colleague Avinash Kaushik.[3] Here, we use a classification to define the key performance indicators, based on the three main metrics of web analytics: the number of unique visitors, the number of visits, and the number of page views, as shown in Figure 3.1.

Number of unique visitors

The number of unique visitors to a website is the basic unit of measurement of a website or a web page in general (Facebook, Google). Typically, visitors who come on a site can view one or more pages, during one or more visits. The standard time unit for counting visitors is generally a month. The calculation of the real audience of a site is based on the concept of "unique visitors," which refers to the number of unique visitors in a given period – usually one month, but the unit of time may vary depending the requirements of the analysis. For example, during the end-of-year holiday season it will be a week – the two weeks leading up to Christmas are a crucial period for merchants on the Internet. During this period, they seek to maximize the traffic to their site, the number of unique visitors, and the number of buyers.

The number of unique visitors is an important measure but it is essential to treat it with caution. Different audience measurement tools can give different numbers, so one should not consider the value of the number of unique visitors in absolute terms, but in relative terms over time. Similarly, an increase in the number of unique visitors from one period to another does not mean that your digital marketing is more effective. Of course, if you work in the media field, where the business model involves development of the audience (to sell advertising space), an increase in the number of unique visitors is a sign of progress, but if you are an advertiser who does not sell anything directly on the Internet and has launched an Internet branding or promotion campaign, an increase in the brand site's traffic is not directly synonymous with success. Indeed, the additional traffic generated may be of poor quality: it may consist of short visits, an abnormally high site "bounce rate," or unique visitors who do not repeat visit from one period to another – all of which are indicators that need to be analyzed for assessing the effectiveness of your campaign.

Although useful and essential, the number of unique visitors is not necessarily an indicator of universal effectiveness. However, it remains an important indicator in the AIDA model for measuring attention and interest, particularly in the context of a temporal evaluation of the performance of a website, Facebook page, and so on. It is important to carefully segment visitors by traffic source, origin, visitor navigation route, and so on – information that can optimize the management and hence the effectiveness of digital marketing.

Number of visits

The number of visits may seem an indispensable metric, but in fact it is not. If, for example, a single visitor accounted for all the visits to a site, there would be little chance that your sales and image objectives would be attained. Consequently, it is useful without being universal: the number of visits should increase in accordance with the number of unique visitors and, depending on the case, you will aim to maximize or rather optimize the number of visits and/or the number of page views per unique visitor. A loyal audience, which returns several times a month, is certainly useful for a media site, but is probably less so for a brand website that does not have a loyalty program, where one or two visits are often sufficient to find the desired information. It is thus evident that the performance indicators used should be directly aligned with the objectives. To do this, we invite the reader to always refer to the recommendations for determining KPIs.

Number of page views

In a trivial way, the number of page views is the number of times a page has been viewed. In the early days of the web, a page consisted mainly of text. The emergence of websites and content that are more interactive (for example through flash animations) and personalized (for example information transmitted by Google Maps with Ajax technology) forced the publishers

57

The different types of metrics and KPIs available: "quantitative" vs. "qualitative"

of web analytics solutions to configure different types of available content: ranging from PDF files to podcasts, flash and Ajax animations, and video. It is also important not to confuse the number of hits and the number of page views. The complexity and richness of existing sites can generate dozens of hits per page, and from the standpoint of the analysis of marketing effectiveness, the number of page views is clearly the metric of most interest. As such, an increase or decrease in the number of page views does not mean that a site's performance has improved or deteriorated; it all depends, once again, on the site's business model. A news media site, one of whose objectives is expanding the audience in order to sell advertising, will seek to increase the number of page views; while an e-merchant who wishes to optimize the conversion rate will, in some cases, endeavor to present the product or most suitable offering as quickly as possible to the visitor, who will then be able to buy it with a minimum of clicks.

The three basic metrics of web analytics, the number of visitors, the number of visits, and the number of page views, are far from sufficient to fully evaluate the impact of digital actions. Other indicators or KPIs developed from these metrics are also available, and we describe these in relation to the AIDA model. Without seeking to be exhaustive, the aim is to provide some initial thoughts to allow advertisers to organize their KPIs for relatively traditional marketing objectives: attracting attention, arousing interest, creating desire and preferences, and promoting action (purchase or repeat purchase).

Web analytics KPIs for measuring attention in the AIDA model

Attracting attention is the first step in the AIDA model. In other words, making sure that people are paying attention to you, that they come and "knock on your door," that they visit your site or Facebook page.

Number of visitors

The number of visitors is a typical indicator for measuring impact in terms of attention. It is a quantitative indicator of audience size, and therefore of attention. It must be monitored and evaluated dynamically and should be assigned the right importance, since everything depends on the site's business model. The greater the value placed on audience figures, as with media and news sites, the more strategic the visitor numbers KPI will be. Similarly, websites and Facebook fan pages can serve as a sounding board for radio or TV advertising campaigns. Today, many of these regularly direct people who are interested to the advertiser's website or the fan page. In this instance, the growth in the numbers of visitors before, during and after the campaign is a good indicator of attention and the interest aroused by the campaign and thus of its potential effectiveness. In fact, we worked on this very subject for a car advertiser in the early 2000s. At that time, it was simply a matter of looking at the relationship between the potential impact of the brand's new TV campaigns and the number of visitors and the number of new visits to the advertiser's website. Clearly, such a relationship exists, and the "best campaigns" tend to generate a higher number of visits to the website. More recently, the same type of statistical analysis has been used to check the impact of offline campaigns (TV and radio) on the advertiser's Facebook page. Apart from the number of visitors, it is interesting here to follow *changes in the mix of the keywords typed* into search engines, both with regard to spontaneous searches and to sponsored links and ads. The more the name of the brand, product or campaign generates new visits, the greater the attention paid to the campaign. Systematic benchmarking of campaigns will allow the digital manager to evaluate the effects and effectiveness of campaigns.

Share of first and repeat visitors

Directly related to the number of visitors, the share of first and repeat visitors are two important indicators of effectiveness. When a recruitment campaign produces the desired effects, it may, for example, increase the number of first visitors to the site. But it is also important to look at the quality of these new first visitors. Did they subsequently return to the website or page? Did they stay long enough on the site? Which recruitment sources of these first visitors are the most profitable? Such questions are essential if one is to go beyond the number of visitors and put this figure into perspective and hence make better use of it.

59

The different types of metrics and KPIs available: "quantitative" vs. "qualitative"

Web analytics KPIs for measuring the stages of interest and desire in the AIDA model

Once visitors have been "attracted," it is necessary to establish their real interest. Some people may claim that a visit alone is a sign of interest, but at this stage it is important to be more demanding. Specialists will appreciate here the parallel we are trying to make between indicators measuring interest (in the sense of the AIDA model) and "quality of visit" indicators, well known to practitioners of web analytics. Depending on the case, there are many indicators of interest that can also be used for estimating "desire" or preference or acclaim in the AIDA model, which is why we prefer to address them simultaneously. Once again, web analytics experts will be able to recognize a number of indicators commonly used to measure the quality of the content.

Average duration of the visit

The average duration of the visit is the first interesting indicator. At first sight, the more time a visitor spends on your site, the more they are interested. This reasoning is logical enough, but needs to be qualified. It is still important to establish that people find what they are looking for, and that a long visit is not, on the contrary, a counterindicative sign with regard to the principle of maximizing time spent on a site. Typically, a registration or sale form should help maximize the quality of information collected in relation to the time spent. From this standpoint, rather than simply measuring the average duration of the visit in absolute terms, one needs to look at it in relative terms and see how it changes over time. Another caveat is that in the case of a visit to a single page, such as blogs or Facebook pages, the duration of the visit is zero. Thus, the duration of visit indicator should only be used when it is really relevant.

Number of visits per visitor

The number of visits per visitor is simply the ratio between the number of visits and the number of visitors over the reference period. Given the methodological imperfections of web analytics tools, the evolution of this indicator should be followed from one period to another, rather than considering its value only at a given time. In particular, attention should be paid to the stability of its value from one period to the next, which overall is an indicator of visitor loyalty. Loyalty will tend to increase insofar as the content of the site or page is regularly updated. When setting performance goals, it is important to bear this in mind: without additional content, there is little chance of increasing loyalty to the site and thus the number of visits per visitor.

Average number of page views per visit

In the same vein as the previous indicator, the average number of page views per visit, calculated as the ratio between page views and the number of visits, is an indicator of the quality of the content and the level of interaction generated by the site. The larger the number of page views per visit, the greater the interest of the site to its visitors. However, as mentioned for the length of visit indicator, it does not seem to be of any great value in absolute terms. Everything depends on the site, the objectives, and the section of the site visited. Our experience suggests that four to six pages, on average, are viewed per visit.

Most visited pages

The most visited pages are generally excellent indicators of visitors' interests. Their analysis is used to evaluate the differences that may exist between the objectives of a digital marketing plan and the interests revealed by visits and visitors' interaction with some content rather than other content. Typically, for an e-commerce site, the most visited product pages usually generate the site's highest sales. Similarly, the pages that are most visited or "read" on a site, such as that of the financial newspaper FT.com, give a good idea of the interests of the readership. The same goes for the most visited pages of a brand site, which reveal the drivers of visitors' interests and preferences. For example, a recent analysis[4] carried out using traffic data from the movie website Allocine.fr showed the usefulness of indicators of the most viewed film and trailer pages. These proved to be excellent indicators of the popularity and success of film on release in cinemas. The authors of the study thus confirm the value of "proxy" indica-

61

The different types of metrics and KPIs available: "quantitative" vs. "qualitative"

tors on the web for estimating and predicting markets. The same type of analysis has since been extended to other sectors, such as video games and mass retail. These confirm the quality and usefulness of the most visited pages indicator for understanding the interests and preferences revealed by Internet users' visits and behavior. We would encourage the reader to consider incorporating this into the development of predictive models of the effects and effectiveness of digital marketing plans.

In the case of Facebook, it is the number of exposures or clicks on posts (engaged users) that give an indication of interest in the content. Facebook further extends statistics on measures of interest and preference on its fan pages (the desire stage in the AIDA model) by making indicators of unique visitors (reach) and virality of content available on the page. Two indicators of virality coexist. The first refers to *people talking about* the post: they may "like" the content, share it, and comment on it. The second, *engagement,* can be calculated by dividing the number of people who have "talked" about a post by the number of fans (see Figure 3.2).

Bounce rate

The bounce rate is one of the most popular indicators, made famous by Google Analytics among others. The bounce rate measures the visits to a single page on a site. Intuitively, the higher its percentage, the more quickly visitors leave the site after their arrival, and hence the less they find of interest there. Consequently, the site manager will endeavor to minimize the bounce rate. But once again, this needs to be qualified, since in the case of a single page website, or in the case of pages that are intended to provide information quickly (for example, a phone number on the "contact" page), minimizing the bounce rate is not an objective in itself. That said, it is still reasonable to assume that the lower the bounce rate, the more visitors will find the content of interest and will develop a preference for the brand and the product. Three different bounce rates are usually calculated: the rate for the site as a whole, the page rate, and the traffic source rate:

- *Overall bounce rate of the site:* this is calculated by dividing the number of visits to a page by the total number of visits to the site. If

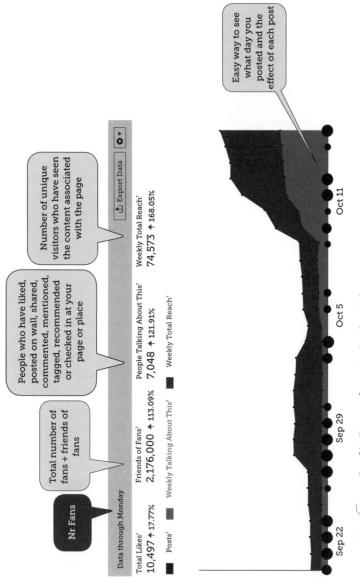

FIGURE 3.2 Example of indicators from Facebook Insights

63

The different types of metrics and KPIs available: "quantitative" vs. "qualitative"

the aim of the site is to develop the brand relationship and enhance interest in and preference for the brand, it is important to track its bounce rate and evaluate its evolution, while trying to benchmark[5] similar sites. So each site, or rather site category, has its own level of bounce rate. As so often on the Internet, it is important to qualify or rather contextualize the results of the analysis, so as to better assess performance and thus set realistic goals. A study by KISSmetrics[6] in 2011 shows that the average bounce rate is around 40% and the number of pages per visit 4.6. Focusing on mean bounce rates by type of site, the analysis shows that these vary between 10% and more than 90%. Service sites, portals (Yahoo!, MSN), and some e-commerce sites have generally low bounce rates. In contrast, sites with a single page (the famous landing pages) have the highest bounce rates. Figure 3.3 shows the averages by industry.

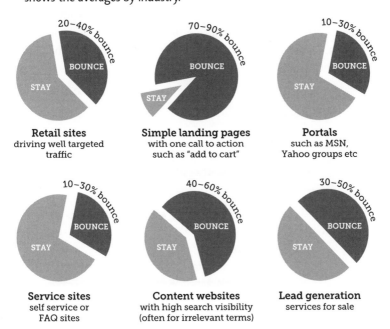

Retail sites
driving well targeted traffic

Simple landing pages
with one call to action such as "add to cart"

Portals
such as MSN, Yahoo groups etc

Service sites
self service or FAQ sites

Content websites
with high search visibility (often for irrelevant terms)

Lead generation
services for sale

FIGURE 3.3 / Average bounce rates by industry

Source: KISSmetrics.[6]

- *The page bounce rate:* this is calculated by dividing the number of times the page has been seen only once by the number of times the page has been the homepage. This indicator is especially important when it concerns content that is likely to directly enhance interest and preferences or, in the case of an a e-commerce site, lead to action and/or purchasing. So, carefully track your site's hot content pages. If they have a high bounce rate, either the content is not sufficiently interesting or the ergonomics is not optimal, and visitors are not taking the time to linger.
- *The traffic source bounce rate:* this is calculated by dividing the number of visits on one page of the campaign by the total number of visits generated by the campaign. This indicator should be systematically analyzed for your campaigns. Indeed, there is too little analysis of the quality of incoming traffic, with much analysis going no further than the number of visits or visitors, indicators that are certainly relevant for measuring attention, but are too limited to fully take into account the capacity of a digital campaign to arouse interest, desire and even action. Figure 3.4 shows an illustrative example taken from Google Analytics. It shows the different key KPIs of a given website.

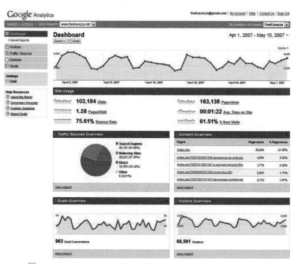

FIGURE 3.4 Change in the bounce rate

Source: Google Analytics.

Web analytics KPIs for measuring the action stage of the AIDA model

It is probably with regard to the action stage that most is expected from the Internet. Remember that we have addressed this point from the beginning of this book: the Internet has long been viewed as the most measurable of media, and the one most able to quantify the impact of a marketing plan. This belief is largely attributable to the indicators made available through web analytics.

Click-through rate

The click-through rate (CTR) is without doubt the most popular indicator. It represents the percentage of visitors who, on being exposed to content (advertisement, web page, keyword, sponsored link) have in fact clicked on the stimulus (in the advertising sense of the term in the terminology of the AIDA persuasion model). Still widely used to evaluate the effectiveness of an advertising campaign, it is now established that even if the CTR is useful for assessing the capacity of a campaign to generate action (visiting a website, registering in a database, purchase), it provides only partial results on full effectiveness in terms of "action." Indeed, some actions are not immediate and can extend over time. Accordingly, the post-view CTR – that is, the percentage of visitors who have visited the site and made a purchase, well after immediate exposure to the message – should also be taken into account to extend the potential effectiveness of a campaign. Some branding or display advertising campaigns, where the main purpose is to keep a brand in people's minds or to change users' perceptions of the brand, must be measured by "going beyond the click" so as to take into account changes in attitude. We will have the opportunity to return to this in more detail below, when we look at the case of more qualitative indicators of effectiveness.

Conversion rate(s)

Conversion rate is the most popular indicator with online retailers, since it measures the percentage of visitors converted into buyers during their visit. Like the CTR, which can measure the efficiency or effectiveness,[7] as appropriate, of exposure to a stimulus, it is reasonable that different conversion rates can coexist for measuring the effectiveness or efficiency of a digital action, and do so from upstream to downstream in the digital conversion funnel or digital conversion process (Figure 3.5). For example, the recruitment stage of the process will endeavor, by means of CTRs (hence conversion rates), to measure the quality of incoming traffic sources (and their associated cost with a view to optimizing the budget invested). In this case, the conversion rate (or CTR) can be regarded as an indicator of efficiency, especially if the ultimate goal of the campaign is to sell, or to ensure that visitors register on a database, or download an information request or appointment form. The digital marketing manager will then update the conversion rates specific to each objective and each stage of the digital funnel.

Recruitment
Click-through rate
(efficiency)

Registration
Purchase/Repurchase
Conversion rate
(effectiveness)

Registration
Purchase/Repurchase
Conversion rate
(effectiveness)

FIGURE 3.5 / Digital conversion funnel

Table 3.1 summarizes all the points raised so far. It recaps the KPIs available for each stage of the AIDA model. Without seeking to be exhaustive, it provides the decision-maker with the main elements for thinking about the subject. In all cases, remember that "good KPIs" are primarily those that are relevant to the evaluation of the objectives of the digital marketing campaign.

67

The different types of metrics and KPIs available: "quantitative" vs. "qualitative"

TABLE 3.1 Summary of KPIs from web analytics

Stage of the AIDA model	KPI of the associated web analytics
Attention	Number of visitors First visitors vs. repeat visitors
Interest	Repeat visitors Average duration of visit Average number of visits per visitor Average number of pages seen per visit Most visited pages Bounce rate
Desire	Average number of visits per visitor Average number of pages seen per visit Most visited pages Bounce rate
Action	Click-through rate Conversion rate

Media and advertising KPIs

As the Internet is a new medium, it was initially constructed around the players who "did" the media, namely media sites. Since the business model of these sites is primarily based on the development and particularly the quantification of their audience, it soon became important to measure and quantify this in order to be able to "sell it," or rather sell advertising space to advertisers interested in getting their messages across to this audience.

The quantification of this media audience is mostly based on the same indicators as those derived from web analytics. They are therefore quantitative in nature. We find the same series of metrics, namely the number of unique visitors, number of visits, and duration of visit, which allow the same type of indicators to be constructed as those described above. Audience measurement is based on two methodologies: one, so-called "site-centric," where it is websites that constitute the measurement sample (this is also called web traffic measurement), the other so-called "user-centric," where it is individuals, or rather their navigation and behavior, who are measured, not the sites themselves.

The two types of measure are complementary, thus allowing the reality and diversity of the Internet ecosystem to be captured. In both cases, with regard primarily to measuring audiences, and thus quantifying the number of visitors exposed to a particular site or content, we classify *the indicators derived from audience measurements within the category of indicators of the AIDA model measuring attention and/or interest.* Similarly, these indicators of audience size, intuitively enough, yield the initial KPIs of an Internet advertising campaign: the number of impressions generated by the campaign, for example, is none other than the number of times an advertisement (regardless of its format) has been served to the site's visitors. This indicator reveals the level of attention that the campaign is likely to provide the brand or advertiser. Exposure to an ad is not, of course, synonymous with effectiveness in the strict sense of the term, yet it is essential that the user could have noticed it, which is why we use the word "likely;" it is generally estimated that only one in every two banners ads gets noticed. Below, we describe the main audience indicators available.

Audience indicators[8]

- *Unique visitors (UV):* the number of different people who have visited part of a site, a site, a set of sites, the Internet as a whole, or an application during a given month.
- *Unique visitors per day:* the average number of people per day who have visited part of a site, a site, a set of sites, the Internet as a whole, or an application during a given month.
- *Duplication of unique visitors:* the number of visitors common to several sites during a given month.
- *Time spent:* the total number of minutes spent by visitors on part of a site, a site, a set of sites, the Internet as a whole, or an application during a given month.
- *Time spent by unique visitor:* the average number of minutes spent by the visitor on part of a site, a site, a set of sites, the Internet as a whole, or an application during a given month.

- *Visits:* accessing at least one page of a site during a given month. Failure to access new pages on a website, from the same connected device, within a period of 30 minutes, is generally seen as the end of a visit.
- *Coverage (or penetration):* for a given Internet user target, the percentage of this target reached by the site.
- *Affinity:* the percentage of the target reached by a site over the total audience of the site. Affinity can be calculated on unique visitors, page views or minutes, depending on the data available.

Advertising indicators

Once the media plan is constructed, validated by the advertiser, and negotiated with the advertising agencies, the campaign can be launched. The agency then follows the course of the campaign on a daily basis, making changes where necessary so as to optimize it (reparameterization of the reach, exposure capping, targeting, share of voice). At the end of the campaign, unlike with other media, an assessment is systematically carried out for the advertiser, based on predefined objectives. This report uses data from various tools such as ad servers and the web analytics tool.

Diffusion indicators: from ordered impressions to visible impressions

During the diffusion of media plan ordered, the number of ad impressions is tracked. However, an impression can be displayed in an area of the page that is not accessed by the user. In this case, it is more interesting to track the number of impressions actually visible and delivered. The same tracking can also measure the duration of Internet users' exposure to the ad. The number of impressions is therefore typically an indicator of potential attention, in the sense of the AIDA model.

Interaction indicators

The essence of the Internet as an advertising medium is that it allows the user to interact with the ad in a much more extensive way than a simple click. The growing use of event formats and rich media formats is accompanied by the development of indicators able to measure these. Interaction indicators thus stem from these changes in the use of the medium. *Interaction may be defined as the action performed by the Internet user on the advertising format to which they are exposed.* Here, *the click becomes the second level of the interaction with the ad.* The user first interacts when they start playing a video, activate, modify, or mute it, or play with the creation by means of the mouse. It is thus possible to count the number of interacted impressions, and the duration of the interaction. Measurement of the CTR then follows. It is possible to go much further, by calculating a conversion rate, thanks to specific tracking linking the user's actions to their exposure to the ad. This tracking can be done immediately or over time, in two ways: post-click measurements (action following a click on the ad) and post-view measurements (action following exposure to the ad). Post-click analysis and post-view analysis are often contrasted, although, as we see here, they are, in fact, complementary. The tracked action, defined upstream of the campaign, can take different forms, ranging from visiting the site to signing up for a newsletter or making a purchase. This tracking requires the installation of tags on the ad and/or the site. Depending on the specific objectives of the campaign concerned, all these interaction indicators can be considered as indicators of attention, interest, desire, or action in the AIDA model. The digital manager and their agency will seek to define the indicator or indicators that correspond to each stage of the AIDA model.

Advertisement audience indicators on the advertiser's site

Almost all advertising formats are clickable and refer to a website, which is then called the redirect site. Indicators from web analytics can then measure the audience, the traffic generated by the ad, and sales.

Table 3.2 summarizes the key indicators or KPIs available for measuring media and advertising. For each of them, we show the stage or stages of the AIDA model for which they can be used.

TABLE 3.2 Summary of media and advertising KPIs

Stage of the AIDA model	Media and advertising KPIs
Attention	Visits Unique visitors Time spent Coverage Affinity Number of impressions used Number of impressions seen
Interest	Unique visitors Time spent Time spent per unique visitor Coverage Affinity Interaction indicators: clicks, click-through rate
Desire	Interaction indicators: clicks, click-through rate, conversion rate
Action	Interaction indicators: clicks, click-through rate, conversion rate

Consumer metrics and KPIs

Measuring the effects of advertising by these quantitative indicators alone can often prove to be quite limited, particularly in the case of so-called "branding campaigns," where the goal is primarily to call to mind the existence of the brand and/or develop its image. For such campaigns, advertisers increasingly use advertising post-tests, as well as indicators to measure the "buzz" or "engagement" generated by the campaign. These indicators are distinctive in directly involving the Internet user in the implementation of metrics. In other words, whereas quantitative metrics are based on observation of user behavior on a site following exposure to an ad, qualitative metrics seek to understand the effects, reactions, and intentions of users. They are therefore more oriented toward and focused on the individual, the "consumer" so dear to marketers. For this reason, we call them *consumer metrics* and *KPIs*. Typically, in relation to a group of people not exposed to a campaign, these indicators enable each step of the AIDA model to be understood and measured. How many people recall the brand (attention), do they have a better image of it (interest), are they more likely to buy it (desire/action)? Do they talk about it to their acquaintances on social networks (interest/desire)? In short, these are metrics that seek to understand better what goes on "in people's minds" and therefore provide more effective information about the effectiveness of the campaign in terms of qualitative dimensions.

We distinguish two types of qualitative metrics: those obtained by directly questioning people exposed to the campaign and/or online contact point to be evaluated (website, Facebook page) – "asked metrics" – and those collected passively or indirectly by counting the number of times a brand name is mentioned on blogs, forums, and other social networks – "earned metrics." The latter refer to the measurement of buzz or engagement generated by a campaign. We review each of these metrics and the KPIs derived from them.

Direct consumer metrics: asked metrics

Well known to market research professionals, these metrics are all those obtained by directly questioning consumers. Although we will not detail the rules of good practice for posting online questionnaires on the Internet, it is nonetheless appropriate to recall some key principles for maximizing the validity and reliability of the information collected:

1 The first key point is that *the collection should be implemented "hot,"* that is, in the Internet user's natural environment and at the time when exposure to or consumption of interactive content is experienced. This is important because it ensures the validity and reliability of the information collected. Typically, in the case of a website or a Facebook or YouTube page, the collection is done on the site at the end of the visit. For an online advertising campaign, questioning takes place after exposure to the ad by randomly inviting Internet users during their navigation of the site carrying the ad.

2 The second important point is that the questionnaire should be neither too short nor too long, but *should focus on what is essential, while seeking to maximize the quality and comprehensiveness of*

the information collected, and to minimize the collection time so as optimize the experience for the consumer. As well as the accuracy and clarity of the wording of the questions, the ergonomics of the questionnaire is also important. This can have a direct impact on the quality of responses collected, and hence on the measurement of effectiveness.

3 Similarly, on a brand site, a corporate site or e-commerce site, without wanting to influence the impact of the findings, particular attention should be paid to the *quality of the design and the appearance of the questionnaire and the invitation window.* Here, it is the brand that communicates with its visitors, so it is normal that the look and feel of the invitation and questionnaire match the look and feel of the site itself (see the example of the pop-up invitation to answer the questionnaire in Figure 3.6). Paying attention to this point has a direct effect on participation rates and allows the representativeness of the responses collected to be maximized.

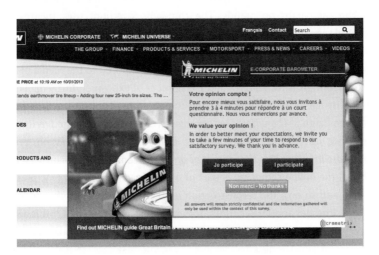

FIGURE 3.6 / Example of a pop-up invitation to answer a website questionnaire

Source: CRM Metrix

Once the responses have been collected (usually to closed questions, to which the possible answers are offered to the respondent when the question is asked), the percentages of responses to each question are calculated. It is these percentages, referred back to a particular respondent base, which will form the main consumer indicators of effectiveness.

We now briefly describe the main consumer indicators used for the evaluation of advertising and websites.

"Consumer" indicators of advertising effectiveness

Advertisers increasingly feel the need to measure the effectiveness of their online campaigns "beyond the click." Indeed, for most consumer brands, whose objective is to remind people of the existence of the brand and develop its image, the only indicator needed is the CTR, which today stands at around 0.03 percent. It has long been established that online advertising has substantial effects on the brand.[9] In the USA, Dynamic Logic was the first company to systematically measure the impact of online campaigns on brands. The company Safecount uses the test/control sampling procedure via continuous recruitment, or "life sampling," which allows visitors to sites used by the online campaign media to be questioned, to isolate the responses of people exposed to the media plan (to ad formats, sites visited), and the number of exposures, thus enabling response curves to be generated and compared to people not exposed to the campaign.[10] *The differences observed on indicators such as advertising memory, advertising recognition, attribution, message association, and purchase intent enable the impact of an online campaign to be measured.* When the online campaign is part of a multimedia campaign (TV, press, radio, and so on), the reconstruction of likely exposures to other media allows Internet and TV synergies, for example, to be evaluated.[11] It is also possible to interview members of an online access panel for implementing studies of advertising effectiveness. As in the first case, to isolate those who are exposed or not exposed to the media plan, it is necessary to have a tool to verify this exposure – as with life sampling, this is generally done by tagging the various ads in the online media plan.

The different types of metrics and KPIs available: "quantitative" vs. "qualitative"

Spurred on by a significant increase in display advertising and its future exponential growth, studies of the effectiveness of online advertising are growing proportionally and are becoming increasingly a matter for specialists (such as CRM Metrix, Dynamic Logic, MetrixLab). Thus, the ideal measurement standard is still to be defined, given the low participation rates recorded in both life sampling and access panels, which seem to suffer less from nonparticipation of Internet users than surveys, but have other shortcomings. A report published in August 2010 in the USA by the Internet Advertising Bureau recommends that all actors "seriously" consider the question of the establishment of standards for the measurement of effectiveness, accepted by the industry as a whole.[12]

Since advertising is essentially persuasive in nature, it is unsurprising that the main stages of the AIDA model are found in the principle consumer indicators of advertising. In turn, these indicators seek to measure attention, interest, desire and action arising from exposure to advertising:

1 *Advertising awareness* and *advertising memory* are the primary indicators for measuring Internet users' attention levels. These indicators are calculated by the percentage of people who say they recall having seen an ad for a particular brand on the Internet. The *advertising recognition indicator*, whether "branded" or "nonbranded" (in the latter case, the originator of the ad is hidden when the ad is presented to respondents), measures the percentage of people who remember seeing the banner. Recognition is generally considered to be an indicator of advertising impact, in the creative sense of the term. Indeed, recognition may be high, but if the link or attribution to the brand is low, memory and awareness will not be as high. In this case, the campaign will have poorly exploited its full impact potential for attracting the attention of Internet users.

2 One of the most common indicators for assessing interest in an ad is *approval* or the percentage of people who say they "like" the ad. Other so-called "diagnostic" indicators are better for assessing the attrac-

tiveness of the ad and mark the extent to which it may be intrusive, repetitive, humorous or involving.

3 The stages of desire and action of the AIDA model are typically measured by indicators of *purchase intent*, intent to find out more, and intent to talk about it to one's friends. To gain a better understanding of the desire and brand preference induced by the ad, it is not uncommon to measure changes in brand image indicators by comparing perceptions between people exposed and not exposed to the media campaign.

Effectiveness is evaluated in "absolute" terms by comparing a campaign's impact scores between those exposed and not exposed to the ad, but also in "relative" terms in relation to standards that take into account the product category, investment level, and advertising formats (banner sizes, types of animation). We will return later to the analyses carried out on the basis of these effectiveness indicators, by means of examples.

Table 3.3 summarizes the main "consumer" indicators of advertising effectiveness.

TABLE 3.3 Summary of consumer KPIs for advertising effectiveness

Stage of the AIDA model	"Consumer" indicators of advertising effectiveness
Attention	Advertising awareness Advertising memory Advertising recognition
Interest	Liking Diagnostic indicators
Desire/action	Purchase intent indicator Request for information indicator Recommendation indicator Brand image indicators

"Consumer" indicators of the effectiveness of a website

In the same way as for advertising, the quantitative metrics derived from web analytics are insufficient to fully assess the effectiveness of a website. For example, how can one really grasp the effects on the brand image of a visit to a brand website? Typically, these branding effects cannot be taken into account and measured by quantitative indicators. As we have seen, these studies invite visitors to the site to answer a questionnaire (on entering and/or leaving the site – the so-called "test/control" methodology) and allow one to go beyond the ergonomic aspects the visitor's experience and to understand the satisfaction levers of the experience and impact of the visit in terms of interest, desire and action (in the AIDA sense of the terms). Known as "attitudinal web analytics" as opposed to web analytics, they provide the "why" of visits to the site and also allow better use of the place and role of the website in the digital strategy of the brand or company (for corporate sites). For example, from the analysis of the aggregated database of 102 online studies, Florès and Volle[13] show that the brand website is a marketing tool that can improve several performance indicators – particularly purchase intention and attitude toward the brand – and can initiate an exchange with the best clients. The same type of analysis conducted from the database of the e-corporate barometer confirms the impact of the corporate site on the company's image.[14] Figure 3.7 shows the six dimensions of the effectiveness of a website.[15]

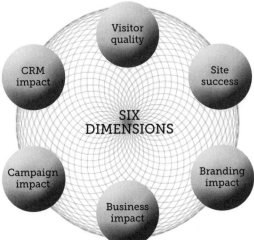

FIGURE 3.7 The six dimensions of effectiveness of a website

Source: CRM Metrix.

The six dimensions of effectiveness of a website allow one to keep abreast of and evaluate the operation of the site as a whole, covering variously the characterization of its visitors (visitor quality: in sociodemographic terms, but also and especially in terms of economic and influence value) and their origin, the (online and offline) impact of recruitment campaigns, perception of the site (through overall and specific measures of satisfaction with its content, appearance, and ease of navigation), and the relational, branding and business impact of the visit on the visitor. Table 3.4 summarizes the main consumer indicators for measuring the effectiveness of a website.

TABLE 3.4 Summary of consumer KPIs for website effectiveness

Stage of the AIDA model	Consumer indicators of the effectiveness of a website
Attention	First visitors vs. repeat visitors Origin of visits: online or offline
Interest	Visitor quality: sociodemographic profile, economic value, influence value Visit motivations Achievement of the main purpose of the visit Opinion of the brand before the visit Satisfaction Revisit intent Recommendation intent
Desire	Revisit intent Recommendation intent Change of opinion regarding the brand
Action	Purchase intent Recommendation intent Purchase during and/or after the visit (on the site or in a store)[16]

"Indirect" consumer metrics: "earned metrics"

Indirect consumer metrics or earned metrics (earned in the sense that consumers have spontaneously mentioned the brand, posted a comment, "tweeted" its name, "liked" its Facebook page, or keyed its name into a search engine) are generally collected by counting, for

The different types of metrics and KPIs available: "quantitative" vs. "qualitative"

example, the number of times that a brand is mentioned on blogs, forums and other social networks, or by analyzing "sentiment" or the tone of comments so as to ascertain the value of conversations about a brand: are they positive, neutral or negative? Other, more advanced kinds of semantic analyses examine the images associated with the brands under discussion. Why focus on these metrics in assessing the effectiveness of digital marketing? The answer is relatively simple. Since the take-off of Web 2.0 in 2006, with the arrival of blogs and, more recently, social networks like Facebook and Twitter, brands and marketing more generally have entered a new era in which the consumer is more active than ever and able to express their opinion and share it with their peers – in short, influencing their peer group with regard to the brands and products they buy, consume, like, and hate. Since then, word of mouth or "buzz" on the Internet has become the new hot topic for marketing and advertising professionals. Alongside campaigns in traditional media, many brands now endeavor to activate buzz on the Internet through viral marketing campaigns. The objective is often to disseminate brand messages by activating influential consumer and opinion leader networks.[17] It is therefore natural that brand managers and their agencies are interested in the impact of their digital campaigns, and their campaigns in general, by tracking and estimating the degree of commitment generated by the campaign. While the notion of "commitment" is commonly used in advertising jargon to designate the active participation of consumers in the life of the brand, it takes on a different dimension on the Internet. As we have already mentioned with regard to quantitative indicators of advertising effectiveness, the proliferation of rich media formats is accompanied by the development of interaction indicators, also known as "commitment" indicators. At present, there is no consensus on the definition of these indicators, nonetheless it is important not to confuse them. Interaction may be viewed as referring to the action performed by the Internet user on the advertising format to which they are exposed. It is part of engagement, but is not its only component. The measurement of engagement may also include exposure time to the ad or the actions taken following exposure (making a comment in the brand website or a blog, transferring the content of an advertising message to a third party, or relaying information on social networks). To enrich the measurement of engagement, it is also legitimate, and necessary, to take into account metrics related to the brand's e-reputation. Like engagement, *e-reputation* is a recent concept, whose measurement indicators are not yet subject to generally accepted consensus by market actors. It covers all content that directly or indirectly affects the reputation or status of an individual, a company or, more generally, a brand, and contributes to its image. Managing its e-reputation is therefore a very real and well-documented challenge for a brand. However, there are many possible ways of measuring e-reputation, with varying degrees of precision and comprehensiveness. These include:

- crawling and lexical/semantic analysis, which elucidate the array of meanings associated with a brand
- counting, which measures the number of mentions of a brand in tweets and blogs and the number of fans on its Facebook page
- analysis of conversations on forums and blogs
- studies of search requests by Internet users regarding the brand.

Whatever the tools used, the metrics obtained allow indicators to be constructed that measure the *noise* or *buzz of a brand* (the number of mentions, tweets and searches, and the number of fans), *sentiment*, the *tonality* or *tone of conversations* around the brand (positive, neutral, negative), and the *images* and *expression territories* associated with the brand. Each of these indicators provides information on the levels of impact and commitment generated by campaigns. As with other indicators, we have positioned them in relation to the AIDA model in Table 3.5. As was the case with the other types of indicator, they may be used variously for one or more stages of the AIDA model, depending on the objectives of the campaign.

81

The different types of metrics and KPIs available: "quantitative" vs. "qualitative"

TABLE 3.5 Summary of "indirect" consumer KPIs for earned metrics

Stage of the AIDA model	"Indirect" consumer indicators (earned metrics)
Attention	Number of mentions of the brand on blogs and forums Number of tweets Number of brand queries on a search engine Number of fans
Interest	Number of mentions of the brand on blogs and forums Number of tweets Number of brand queries on a search engine Number of fans
Desire	Measurement of sentiment (positive, neutral, negative)/tonality Images and associated expression territories
Action	Measurement of sentiment (positive, neutral, negative)/tonality

As is the case for indicators derived from web analytics, one fully appreciates their value over time by comparing changes in performance levels before, during, and after campaigns. For example, Figure 3.8 shows the evolution of interest in parties of the Right and Left, before and during the 2007 French presidential election. The interest indicator used is simply the number of queries keyed into Google.

The number of searches indicator is interesting because it reveals, for example, that by aggregating interest in political parties on a Left/Right basis, we see that the contest was still very open between the two sides until September 2005. After that, interest in the Right, in the broad sense, predominates.

Complementarity of quantitative and qualitative indicators

Over and above the specific characteristics of existing metrics, whether quantitative or qualitative, it is essential to update, adapt, and choose metrics that are best able to measure the objectives of a digital campaign or marketing plan.

We cannot emphasize enough that it is the marketing objectives that should determine the updating of suitable KPIs. As we have explained, the fact that the Internet produces so many metrics does not necessarily mean that

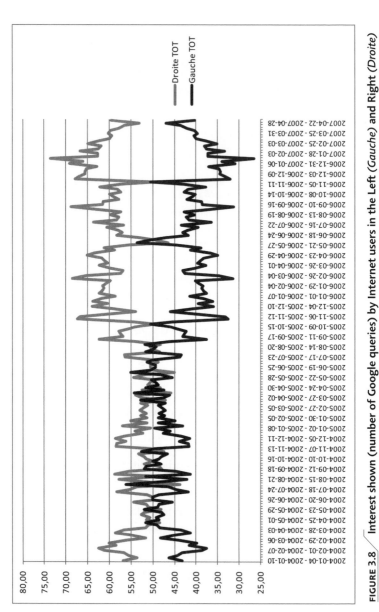

FIGURE 3.8 Interest shown (number of Google queries) by Internet users in the Left (*Gauche*) and Right (*Droite*) in the 2007 presidential election

85

The different types of metrics and KPIs available: "quantitative" vs. "qualitative"

it is more "measurable," or that the "free" metrics and indicators it produces will always be useful for demonstrating its impact. This caveat applies to each stage of the AIDA model. By way of example, attract attention, the first stage of the AIDA model, can be measured (depending on the type of digital point of contact: website, Internet advertisement, Facebook page) through quantitative or qualitative metrics or both. The number of visitors to a website may well serve as a measure of attention. Advertising memory or brand awareness following exposure to a digital campaign can serve the same purpose. Similarly, the interest aroused, the second stage of the AIDA model, can be measured by the CTR, the most preferred and commonly used quantitative metric. Yet the CTR alone is unable to fully measure the exposure potential of a display banner ad campaign, for example. The memory created and the interest aroused in the brand are important and necessary qualitative metrics for best measuring the impact of a campaign. It is therefore in the alignment of metrics and measures with the objectives, and not the reverse, that the key to success lies. Without this adjustment process upstream of the implementation of the digital marketing plan, it is difficult to confidently assess and evaluate the effects and hence the effectiveness of digital marketing. The same discipline should dictate the implementation of digital marketing performance indicators, so as to update KPIs capable of fully capturing, managing, and advancing the achievement of the objectives of the plan implemented. Thus, we are at once alerting and appealing to actors in the marketing profession. It is a matter of urgency that they reappropriate the web and its tools so as to make interactive marketing the main weapon in their armory for conquering and retaining markets. The danger they face is that web financiers and technicians are interested only in "counting" rather than really measuring and, in so doing, forget about consumer effectiveness indicators. The web is above all a social phenomenon (social networks are the best example of this), and the future of digital marketing and marketing in general depends on taking into account and sharing quantitative and qualitative effectiveness indicators that are understood and used by everyone. Measuring is not easy, but it is the price to be paid if digital and the entire marketing profession are to have, and continue to have, an ever brighter future ahead of them.

How to Measure Digital Marketing

TABLE 3.6 Quantitative and qualitative metrics and KPIs

Marketing objectives	Stage of the AIDA model	Paid media (advertising)
Awareness	Attention	Visits Unique visitors Time spent Reach Affinity Number of impressions served Number of impressions seen Advertising awareness Advertising memory Advertising recognition
Image	Interest	Unique visitors Time spent Time spent per unique visitor Reach Affinity Interaction indicators: clicks, CTR Liking indicator Diagnostics indicators
	Desire	Interaction indicators: clicks, click-through rate, conversion rate Purchase intent indicator Information request indicator Recommendation indicator Brand image indicators
Purchase/repurchase	Action	Interaction indicators: clicks, click-through rate, conversion rate Purchase intent indicator Information request indicator Recommendation indicator Brand image indicators

85

The different types of metrics and KPIs available: "quantitative" vs. "qualitative"

Owned media (sites)	Earned media (buzz/engagement)
Number of visitors First visitors vs. repeat visitors Origin of visits: online or offline	Number of mentions of the brand name on blogs and forums Number of tweets Number of brand searches on a search engine Number of fans
Repeat visitors Average length of visit Average number of visits per visitor Average number of page views per visit Most visited pages Bounce rate Quality of visitors: sociodemographic profile, economic value, influence value Visit motivations Achievement of the main purpose of the visit Opinion of the brand before the visit Satisfaction Revisit intent Recommendation intent	Number of mentions of the brand name on blogs and forums Number of tweets Number of brand searches on a search engine Number of fans
Average number of visits per visitor Average number of page views per visit Most visited pages Bounce rate Revisit intent Recommendation intent Change of opinion about the brand	Measurement of sentiment (positive, neutral, negative)/ tonality Images and associated expression territories
Click-through rate Conversion rate Purchase intent Recommendation intent Purchase during and/or after the visit (on the site or in a store)	Measurement of sentiment (positive, neutral, negative)/ tonality

Before we close this chapter on the metrics and KPIs pertaining to the effectiveness of digital marketing, Table 3.6 summarizes the various quantitative and qualitative metrics and the KPIs available for measuring and evaluating the impact of digital marketing actions, for each stage of the AIDA model: from the creation to the maintenance of awareness (attention), by way of the development of brand interest, image, and preference (interest, desire), through to action, namely purchase, repurchase, or recommendation to a friend or family member. We also attempt to classify all the indicators for each of the "major media categories" to be measured: paid, owned, and earned media (POEM).

We are often asked about the ideal number of KPIs to use. In response, we say, with a smile, "neither too many nor too few." Indeed, there is no single magic indicator that by itself can encapsulate the performance of a digital point of contact. Such an approach is particularly well represented by the net promoter score,[18] which, in the space of just five years, has become the marketing performance indicator of many companies, including General Electric. Can one really measure the performance of a company, website, or other online point of contact by subtracting the number of "critics" from the number of "promoters"? At best, this indicator can serve as a diagnosis proxy of the health of a brand, but a great many serious scientific studies have already revealed its limitations and restrictions.[19] More importantly, a study conducted in December 2011 by the World Federation of Advertisers[20] among its members tells us about the ideal number of KPIs to use. This study suggests that the average is between 5 and 10; 52 percent of digital marketing managers of large groups believe that the ideal number of KPIs lies between 5 and 10, while 24 percent believe the number should be between 10 and 15. Thus, there is not necessarily an "ideal" number of KPIs, since everything depends on tracking requirements and objectives. Nonetheless, bear in mind that "the best is often the enemy of good."

Having now defined and explained the various quantitative and qualitative KPIs, in Chapters 4–6, we will give examples of the application of these metrics and indicators to the different types of media contacts:

87

The different types of metrics and KPIs available: "quantitative" vs. "qualitative"

paid, owned and earned media. The aim is to illustrate, by means of examples, how these KPIs are put into practice and used.

Key points

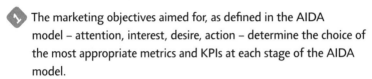

1. The marketing objectives aimed for, as defined in the AIDA model – attention, interest, desire, action – determine the choice of the most appropriate metrics and KPIs at each stage of the AIDA model.

2. The various metrics and KPIs derived from web analytics, advertising, and the reactions of consumers themselves allow the effectiveness of digital marketing to be evaluated.

Notes

1   Eckerson, W. (2006) *Performance Dashboards*, Wiley.
2   For more information, see www.netpromoter.com. We will critically reconsider this KPI later on.
3   Kaushik, A. (2009) *Web Analytics 2.0: The Art of Online Accountability and Science of Customer Centricity*, John Wiley & Sons.
4   Belvaux, B. and Florès, L. (2010) "The use of web proxies for predicting markets: an application to the film market," *Decisions Marketing*, 57: 9–18.
5   Google Analytics provides benchmarks, which are of course only a relative value, since it is difficult to know how they are calculated (which specific sites are aggregated). But they are still useful, especially over time. Interactive agencies must also be able to guide their clients on the subject.
6   KISSmetrics (2011) The 2011 Web Analytics Review, http://blog. kissmetrics.com/2011-web-analytics-review/?wide=1.
7   We refer the reader to Chapter 1, where the concepts of efficiency and effectiveness in regard to the objectives of a campaign are defined.
8   Definitions given by the Internet Advertising Bureau (IAB).
9   Hollis, N. (2005) "Ten years of learning of how online advertising builds brands," *Journal of Advertising Research*, June, pp. 255–68.

10 For further information on the life sampling methodology, see www. safecount.net.

11 For example: www.metrixlab.com/solutions/brand-media-advertising-research/cross-media-optimization.

12 For further information, see the IAB report at www.iab.net/about_ the_iab/recent_press_releases/press_release_archive/press_release/ pr-080510.

13 Florès, L. and Volle, P. (2005) "Relationship potential and brand website impact on marketing performance", *Decisions Marketing*, special issue on marketing performance, 40: 39–50.

14 For further information, see www.journaldunet.com/ebusiness/ marques-sites/dossier/071005-barometre-sites-corporate/.

15 The concept of the six dimensions of the effectiveness of a website was developed by CRM Metrix.

16 The ROPO concept, research online, purchase offline, highlights the impact of visits to a site on in-store sales. We return to this topic with examples for measuring the owned media impact of websites. For more information, see www.iabfrance.com/?go=edito&eid=1.

17 For a review, see Keller, E. and Berry, J. (2003) *The Influentials: One American in Ten Tells the Other Nine How to Vote, Where to Eat, and What to Buy*, Free Press.

18 For further information, see www.netpromoter.com.

19 See, for example, Keiningham, T., Cooil, B., Andreassen, T.W. and Aksoy, L. (2007) "A longitudinal examination of net promoter and firm revenue growth," *Journal of Marketing*, 71(3): 39–51.

20 www.wfanet.org, December 2011.

4

Measuring paid media

Executive summary

- For most brands, "paid" advertising or communication has always been one of the most natural ways of raising awareness. This is also the case for digital media. Yet, while the monitoring of effectiveness is well established for advertising in "offline" media, it is not always implemented on the Internet.

- Limited solely to tracking "quantitative" indicators of coverage (number of impressions and visits, click-through rates), the branding effects are often ignored (awareness, image, purchase intention). These effects are, however, greatly magnified with cross-media campaigns, where it becomes crucial to measure and evaluate them.

Measuring paid media: the most natural measurement for a brand

Brands have always made a point of talking about themselves in the media. The major media of TV, press, radio, and billposting have long been the best allies of brands for launching a new product, repositioning a product line, or simply reminding customers of their existence. Very early on, an industry emerged and a new profession was born, that of advertising. Advertising groups developed around the various skills of the profession, ranging from buying space to media planning, by way of strategic planning and creation. Today, agencies have specialists in the various subdivisions of advertising and for different media, but an underlying trend has revolutionized the advertising market, namely the upsurge of digital media. All the major groups have now incorporated digital into their skill sets, and it is "interactivity" that drives the advertising profession. Measuring paid media and more generally advertising on the Internet is therefore a relatively natural approach for advertisers. At an early stage, some of them, such as P&G, which spends more than 10 percent of its revenue on advertising, became interested in optimizing their advertising expenditure by testing the effectiveness of their advertisements both prior to the launch of the media campaign – through ad pre-testing – and afterwards – through ad post-testing – or throughout the year by monitoring the impact of ads on all the brands in a market ("ad tracking"). These test practices were developed long before the emergence of the Internet, and nowadays traditional players in advertising effectiveness measurement, such as Ipsos or Millward Brown, are competing with younger, "digital" players like MetrixLab. With digital often accounting for more than 15 percent of advertising expenditure, it is no longer possible to ignore its importance and effects, considered individually and in synergy with other media. We will illustrate the implementation of advertising KPIs by taking into account different types of digital media, from traditional banners on a portal site like Yahoo! through to the effect of searches, or of YouTube in terms of branding and the impact of advertising on Facebook, as well as the combined effects of cross-media campaigns.

Recap: the main "quantitative" indicators of online advertising

Having identified the main quantitative indicators of advertising in Chapter 3, here we only consider the main KPIs available by putting them into perspective with regard to the AIDA model. Remember that from the moment of launching a campaign, the agency can monitor its progress in real time, using data from the ad server. Indicators pertaining to the roll-out of the campaign are then available, namely the *number of impressions* and *interaction indicators*, of which the click-through rate (CTR) is the best known. Since rich media have allowed the development of increasingly involving formats, other interaction indicators may also be available even before the CTR itself. In addition to ad server data, audience data from the advertiser's site, derived from web analytics, can enrich reach and click data and evaluate the visits and the number of visitors that the campaign has succeeding in attracting to the site. As a reminder, Table 4.1 summarizes the main quantitative indicators for assessing the impact of the roll-out of an online campaign.

TABLE 4.1 Recap of quantitative indicators for online advertising

Stage of AIDA model	Quantitative indicators for online advertising
Attention	Data from the advertiser's website: Visits Unique visitors Data from the ad server: Number of impressions served Number of impressions seen
Interest	Data from the ad server: Coverage Affinity Interaction indicators: clicks, click-through rate
Desire	Data from the ad server: Interaction indicators: clicks, click-through rate, conversion rates
Action	Data from the ad server: Interaction indicators: clicks, click-through rate, conversion rates

Since the number of clicks alone cannot explain the effects of online advertising, the combination of lower CTRs and increasing online investment provides the key drivers for developing branding effectiveness tests, where the idea is to measure the progressive effects of advertising exposure (in the AIDA sense), so as to raise awareness, enhance image, and boost purchasing and loyalty. Although the purchase of keywords is the main source of expenditure, all professionals agree that the future growth of the market for online advertising will be driven by display and therefore the effect of branding display, especially in synergy with other media. This trend is important because of the exponential rise of real-time bidding (RTB) in advertising that allows both real-time buying and selling of online advertising. Indeed, "ad exchange" networks[1] are currently redefining the digital advertising ecosystem to the point where it is the ad industry at large that may soon experience changes in the way advertising is bought, planned, sold,[2] and evaluated. In this chapter, we will only cover the impact that ad exchanges have on online paid effectiveness. Indeed, thanks to better abilities to efficiently buy media, CTR increases, metrics should be able to demonstrate the impact of RTB advertising on branding.

Measuring the branding effects of online advertising: methodological overview

The study devices put in place for measuring the branding effects of advertising use the so-called "test control" methodology. This allows you to question visitors to the online campaign's media plan sites and, with the systematic tagging of all the online media plan's creations, to isolate the responses of people exposed (sample test) to the media plan (and to the advertising formats of the sites visited) and the number of exposures (enabling response curves to be drawn), so as to compare them with people not exposed (control sample) to this plan. The differences observed on indicators such as ad recognition, attribution, approval, image, and purchase intention allow you to make a diagnosis of the campaign and its impact in terms of branding (awareness, image, purchase/loyalty). Respondents can be recruited either directly on the media plan's sites (live sampling) or from online access panels. In the latter case, responses are collected *at the end* of the roll-out of the media plan, whereas in the case of life sampling, responses are collected throughout the campaign. Figure 4.1 illustrates the study device that allows the effects on people exposed to the media plan and the brand's website to be isolated.

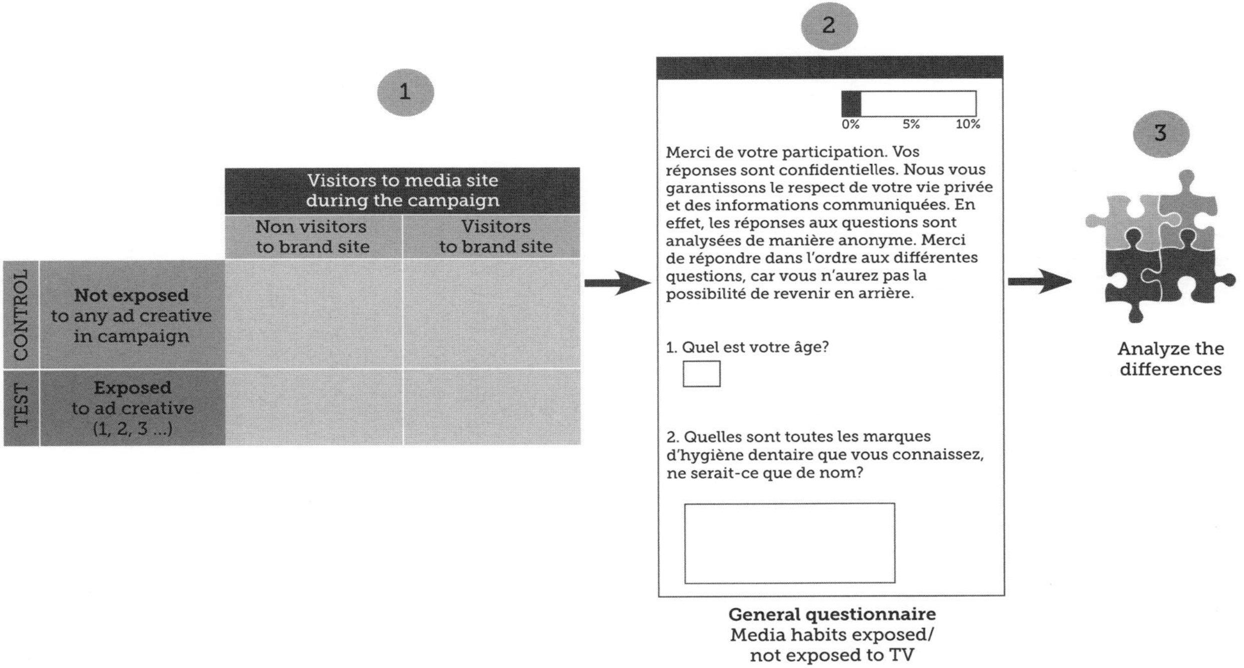

FIGURE 4.1 Cross-media study device: monitoring of online exposure (through tagging) and simulation of the probabilities of exposure to the offline media plan (TV)

Source: CRM Metrix.

Furthermore, when the online campaign is part of a multimedia plan, the reconstitution of probable exposures to other media (especially TV) allows cross-media synergies to be evaluated. International advertisers are increasingly fond of these testing devices, since they provide a good measure of the impact by channel and help evaluate media synergies. We now illustrate these various points through a case study of a mass consumption brand.[3]

An example of effectiveness results for a cross-media campaign

The best way of explaining and illustrating something is often to give a concrete example. Here, we examine the context and main results provided by the qualitative KPIs of the CRM Metrix cross-media post-test.

The context and objectives of the Oral B campaign

The Oral B campaign

Oral B is the undisputed leader of the electric toothbrush market in France, but the brand remains a challenger in the standard toothbrush market, since only 10 percent of French consumers use electric toothbrushes. With Oral B positioned as an upmarket product (the price varies between €20 to €100), the main objectives of the campaign studied were to increase awareness of the brand and the category, by favouring the memorization of the specific advantages and benefits of electric toothbrushes. The ultimate objective was to persuade people to test the product and maximize the purchase by emphasizing promotional offers. To this end, the media campaign, run from February to March 2010, was based on considerable cross-media pressure, relayed in stores, on TV, and online. As Figure 4.2 shows, the digital component of the media plan included a search, display, and emailing device, encouraging consumers to go more often to the mini-site dedicated to the demonstration product and intended to educate consumers and get them to try out the product. More specifically, the online marketing objectives were to increase awareness through more extensive media coverage, as well as to broaden the brand's discourse by means of more developed and demonstrative information content. In this context, the study objectives were to measure the impact of the whole operation, and the online campaign in particular, at each stage of the consumer experience – from media exposure to visiting the website and declared purchase intent.

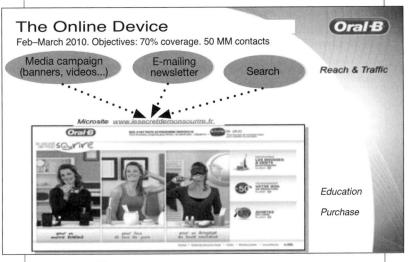

FIGURE 4.2 / The online component of the Oral B campaign, February–March 2010

Source: P&G France.

The main outcomes of the Oral B campaign

Apart from indicators provided by the post-test, the digital manager generally has quantitative indicators supplied by the ad server. These quantitative KPIs include the number of impressions and indicators of "engagement," such as the number of clicks and the CTR, and provide an initial understanding and evaluation of the coverage of the campaign and its efficiency. For reasons of confidentiality, we are unable to give these in the example presented here. However, given the branding objectives assigned to the campaign (awareness, education, testing), only the results of a post-test can allow one to respond to the need to monitor the campaign's branding effectiveness. Figure 4.3 presents the results of the post-test.[4]

Comparisons to norms

Oral-B Internet Campaign (banners and videos)		
	Differences non-exposed vs exposed online (n=513)	Differences vs norms 6D Campaign 360°
Recognition	+++	+
Attribution	++	+
Likability	=	+
Spontaneous awareness	+++	++
Aided awareness	++	+
Purchase intent	=	+

Positive

Significant differences vs non-exposed cell (95%)

FIGURE 4.3 The main impact results of the Oral B campaign

Source: CRM Metrix.

Two levels of interpretation are offered in Figure 4.3: a comparison of impact scores between those exposed and not exposed to the online campaign (1st column), and an evaluation of the impact level of those exposed compared to the norms (2nd column). The analysis here suggests that the campaign clearly achieved its objective of raising awareness. Thanks to the good levels of recognition and attribution, the campaign was "visible" and memorable, and well attributed to the brand. The attention level generated helped significantly increase awareness of the Oral B brand. The purchase intent score was moderate, as it was relatively stable between those exposed and those not exposed, and was slightly above the norm. This is an acceptable result, since it is unsurprising that a single campaign, however creative, could from one day to the next make the majority of French consumers want to try out an electric toothbrush, given that the penetration of the product is currently only around 10 percent. In a way, the problem lies less in the campaign itself and more with the French themselves, who are clearly more resistant than other European populations, for example the Germans, to using an electric toothbrush.

The response curves to exposure to more sustained online advertising (Figure 4.4) confirm the strong potential of the campaign. Only the approval and appreciation levels are unchanged or lower.

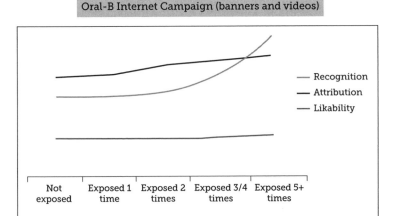

FIGURE 4.4 / Online exposure response curves

Source: CRM Metrix.

Other results that reveal the impact of the multimedia plan, particularly TV, confirm the general impact of the campaign, and especially the additional impact provided by the online campaign, in terms of additional media coverage and the development of awareness and purchase intent. Similarly, visits to the website (following exposure to the online ad) confirm the interest of the site as well as the informative and educational value it provides. Lastly, the post-test confirms the effectiveness of the campaign as a whole, and in particular the specific contribution of the online medium. Moreover, only the post-test is able to respond to the effectiveness monitoring objectives, namely awareness and testing. Indeed, the quantitative indicators from web analytics are unable by themselves to respond to these objectives. We therefore encourage brand managers and digital managers to test their digital campaigns, particularly those whose spend becomes substantial (above €200,000, for example) and which form part of a multimedia plan. They will then be able to understand and evaluate the overall impact of their actions, as well as measure the utility of digital, and thus be in a better position to defend investment in it. Moreover, as online media buying, selling, and serving is getting closer to being integrated in real time, thanks to the rapid growth of RTB made available by ad exchange networks, we believe that the evaluation of branding effects will also need to take place more and more in real time as well, through the integration of real-time survey technology,[5] or more likely through the development of brand effects proxy metrics KPI directly derived from the "big data" made available by the ad exchange networks themselves, which will need to move beyond only reporting "quantitative KPIs." To this end, the development of predictive analytics and machine-learning technologies should soon fuel the development of new branding effects KPI "going beyond the click."

E X P E R T   V I E W P O I N T

Georges Mao
Head of market insights, Southern Europe, Google

Do your large account advertiser clients have a system for measuring the effectiveness of their digital marketing? How do you help them to measure the impact of their actions?

The vast majority of Google's large account advertisers and their advertising agencies always combine digital with a measure of effectiveness, either by recording the number of contacts and clicks of online sales, for reasons of performance, or by using third parties such as panels or institutes, in order to measure the effects linked to their objectives: campaign post-tests, assessment of the impact on in-store sales, and so on.

Google helps its advertiser clients and their agencies to optimize their campaigns, through permanent access to reporting platforms available on product advertising, for example the AdWords platform for keywords. These tools, sometimes in association with analysis by our experts, help make purchasing more effective, to the advantage of cost per click and a more robust performance.

In the context of digital communications and the visibility and reputation objectives, Google offers some of its advertisers post-tests implemented in a cross-media environment (usually on TV and YouTube campaigns), so as to be able, on the one hand, to find complementarity and efficiency "after the facts" compared to various media and, on the other, to better assess the impacts and synergies of the effects provided by the various TV and web exposure combinations, and to identify at what stages of the decision-making process digital communication functions best with the consumers exposed to it.

With regard to cross-channel and indirect flow objectives, Google conducts studies to better allocate the impact of digital touchpoints and their contribution to sales in the physical networks, so as to help advertisers better orient their communications and marketing mix. These studies are implemented in several ways, through modeling (econometrics), geotargeted experiments, and consumer panels.

In terms of measurement, what projects are you working on in order to measure still further the impact and value of digital for your advertiser clients?

Google has three main types of impact measurement projects:

- *Cross-media:* To better measure a given person's media consumption (on four screens: TV, computers, tablets, mobile), allow better planning of content and advertising, and better identify complementarities between TV and online video, particularly in order to reveal the capacity of online video to reach audiences that are difficult to reach through TV.
- *Online to store:* Setting up business cases to better assess the allocation of and return on investment of digital (web, mobile) with regard to sales made in physical networks.
- *New uses:* Identifying new uses by consumers on emerging platforms such as smartphones and tablets, and to identify opportunities in conjunction with key targets for advertisers.

The impact of search on branding

Since advertising investment has historically been attracted by searches, that is, advertising on search engines, primarily Google and its AdWords program, one question is often raised and needs to be answered. Over and above the direct effects in terms of impact that the tracking data of the AdWords program measures perfectly (clicks by keyword, cost per click by keyword, conversion by keyword), what are the effects of advertising by keyword in terms of branding? In other words, apart from the clicks generated by the campaign, can exposure generate impact in terms of awareness, image, interest, and preference (in the sense of the AIDA model)? To answer these questions, MetrixLab, in partnership with Google, has developed an exclusive methodology within the framework of its cross-media post-testing, which can take into account the additional impact effects of searches. The results are significant (Figure 4.5) and confirm that searches are not only a way of making a direct impact (through the direct contact they generate – the click), but also an indirect impact, through the effects on the awareness, image, and consideration

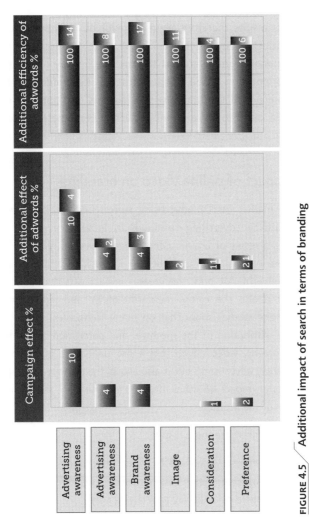

FIGURE 4.5 / Additional impact of search in terms of branding

Source: MetrixLab and Google.

of sponsoring brands. The most significant effects are on advertising awareness and brand awareness, but also on brand image. A less significant effect also occurs on consideration and preference.

These various results therefore argue in favor of a general effect of searches, which goes beyond the click alone, since it impacts the entire conversion funnel, from awareness to purchase by way of image. As well as its orientation based on performance, keyword advertising can complement well the branding mechanisms traditionally set up in cross-media, and can serve the objectives of immediate conversion and branding.

The impact of online video on branding

Whereas the market for TV advertising suffers in times of crisis, the market for display advertising continues to grow at a steady pace, particularly as a result of online video formats. Several recent studies, including those by SmartClip and Nielsen[6] in the USA and MetrixLab[7] in Europe, highlight not only the greater impact of video on display advertising, but also the complementarity of TV and video formats. Specifically, these studies show that on many "consumer" impact KPIs (memory and attribution of the message, and perception of the brand and the campaign), video advertising is not only more effective than traditional display advertising, but it also allows the associated campaign to have a greater impact on other media, particularly TV, strengthening memorization of the message.

Some key figures illustrate these results:

- Among Internet users exposed to video advertising, 37% recalled the message of the campaign (memorization), against 22% for those exposed to conventional display advertising only.
- 28% were able to correctly attribute the advertising message to the brand, against 22% for conventional display advertising.

• The overall perception of the campaign is much more favorable with exposure to the video format. To the question: "What do you think of this campaign as a whole?," 40% of people exposed to the video format responded "very good," against only 14% for the conventional display campaign. The study conducted in 2011 by MetrixLab confirms the capacity of video to strongly enhance the impact and it also reveals that the longer the duration of the video, the greater in general is the retention and enjoyment. It is therefore clear that, in all cases, the quality of the creation is dominant rather than the intrinsically more intrusive nature of the video format.
• In the Nielsen study, the frequency of exposure to the campaign plays a key role for video: the correct attribution of the message rises to 32% after two exposures, and 43% after three exposures to the video ad, whereas this effect is much less pronounced for the display ad.
• Finally, as shown in the example of the Oral B cross-media campaign above, the combined effects of cross-media (online and offline, including TV) reveal the additional impact generated by the Internet, and particularly by video, which further boosts the effects of exposure to classic display alone.

In conclusion, we should point out that the video format cannot by itself guarantee success in terms of the impact of a paid media campaign, but it provides an inherently better means of expression (in the rich media sense of the term) for the creation. As Marie-Pierre Bordet of AACC[8] rightly says:

> Today, in the era of digital, the DNA of success is the same as it has always been: originality, power, meaning, simplicity, conviction, commitment, truth. Those are the creative values associated with original advertising.

This fact is probably best demonstrated by the massive success enjoyed by the recent launch by YouTube of the "TrueView" advertising system, which only charges advertisers for the video advertising "truly viewed" within videos. To date, a good proportion is watched by viewers, although they have the ability to skip the ads. Still, the most creative and engaging ones are watched, which is linked to their creative and original power. So, we believe that video advertising has a tremendous future.

The effects of video advertising virality: the example of YouTube

The impact of offline advertising, in particular TV advertising, is still very strong, but for brands, it is becoming increasingly difficult to stand out – the proliferation of advertising screens, the cost of gross rating point, and increasingly fragmented media consumption by consumers are all reasons for the relative decline of advertising effectiveness. More and more needs to be invested to achieve ever diminishing returns. In this context, digital is increasingly attracting brands, which see in it the possibility of alternating push and pull marketing. In this respect, YouTube is one of the most interesting channels, as the following figures make clear:[9]

- 48 hours of video are uploaded onto YouTube every minute, which represents eight years of content every day; and more than 3 million videos are seen every day
- every week, more than 100 million people socialize on YouTube (through likes, sharing, comments)
- 98 percent of the world's largest advertisers advertise simultaneously on YouTube and Google's display network
- the number of advertisers using YouTube for display advertising increased tenfold from 2010 to 2011.

Furthermore, YouTube is the second largest search engine after Google. In the USA, for example, more than 1.5 million searches are made every day on YouTube. In short, YouTube offers tremendous opportunities for brands to "extend" the life of their TV advertising and, in addition, to develop genuine paid media campaigns on YouTube, maximizing the virality[10] of the campaigns transmitted. There are many campaigns that relay or produce TV movies specially designed to generate buzz.

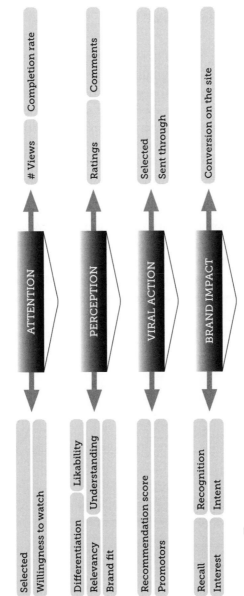

FIGURE 4.6 Quantitative and qualitative KPIs on the impact of YouTube

How to Measure Digital Marketing

"A Hunter Shoots A Bear!"

One recent example is particularly striking: the A Hunter Shoots A Bear! campaign for the Tipp-Ex[11] brand. Produced in 2010 by the agency Buzzman, it was an enormous hit: more than 48 million views on YouTube, shared by over 350,000 people on Facebook during the first three days of the campaign, a tweet every second on Twitter, seen in 217 countries around the world, leading to an increase in sales of more than 30 percent for the brand.[12]

The aim therefore is to develop viral ads. The central issue is to understand what makes an advertisement go viral. A paper from MetrixLab[13] outlines a research study dedicated to understanding why and how an ad goes viral. The quantitative KPIs of YouTube Insights and the qualitative KPIs provided by the different studies (Figure 4.6) provide information about the impact of YouTube videos for each stage of the AIDA model.

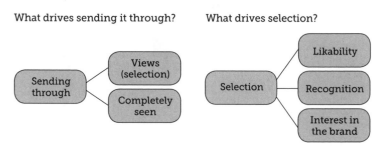

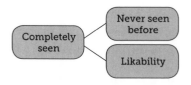

FIGURE 4.7 / Factors explaining the virality of videos on YouTube

The combined analysis of quantitative and qualitative KPIs again confirms that creativity, the ad's likeability and interest or, more generally, positive feelings toward the brand are directly correlated with the greatest virality of YouTube videos (Figure 4.7).

Another study by YouTube,[14] in collaboration with Motorola and General Motors Europe, confirms the *multiplier effect of YouTube videos on branding impact*. Advertising on YouTube affects not only the awareness, image, and purchase intentions, but its effect combined with those of the TV also boosts branding impact.

The impact on sales of online advertising

In these profit-focused times where proof of ROI is required, many questions arise as to the possibility of measuring and demonstrating the direct impact on sales of exposure to online advertising. It is not an easy task. Three main reasons generally limit the implementation of such an exercise:

1 The "measurability" of such an approach: to demonstrate the validity and impact of online advertising, it is still necessary that the investment is measurable and sufficiently "visible" in relation to other expenditure by the brand. Although online investment continues to grow (compared to all media spending) to an average of 15 to 25 percent of all media spending, our recommendation is to measure the online impact for brands that invest sufficiently, especially compared to the other media involved.
2 In order to measure the specific effect of online advertising, one has to be able to "monitor everything," that is, take into account the potential effect of other variables in the mix, such as promotion or, more traditionally, TV advertising. Obtaining a clear overall picture is never easy, especially for mass markets or consumers who are constantly subjected to excessive advertising pressure.
3 The time needed to collect a sufficient history to isolate the effects (by controlling for other variables in the mix) and costs associated with such an exercise. The most suitable brands for this type of exercise are consumer brands, sold in supermarkets and hypermarkets. "Single

source" panels,[15] such as those of IRI in the USA, may therefore be called upon, although their use is limited by the relatively small size of these panels. Consequently, only very large operations for major brands are measurable, and brand managers are often deterred because of the time and costs involved. An alternative to single source panels is to make more systematic use of the databases developed by retailers, available through their in-store purchase programs and loyalty cards. The advantage here is having a larger number of households/consumers whose purchases are measured. The disadvantage is that only purchases made in the stores concerned are taken into account.

An analysis carried out in the USA in October 2011[16] by comScore and dunnhumbyUSA on this type of database (from sales in stores belonging to the retailer Kroger) shows the impact of online advertising on the in-store sales of several consumer products. This study points to a median effect of 21% on in-store sales of several consumer products. This finding is significant and varies within the range from 0 to over 50% (Table 4.2).

TABLE 4.2 Increase of in-store sales of households exposed to online advertising compared to households not exposed

US offline sales lift for CPG brands among households exposed to online advertising compared to households not exposed Studies conducted 2008–10	
Offline sales lift	**Per cent of studies**
0%	17%
1–10%	14%
11–20%	19%
21–30%	10%
31–40%	17%
41–50%	10%
50% et +	14%

Source: comScore AdEffx and dunnhumbyUSA.[16]

In addition, analysis of a sample of products that have benefited from a targeted campaign (in the sense of online "behavioral" advertising, where exposure is based on the affinity profile of visitors to a category or particular brand) shows a median increase in sales of 42 percent – double the effect observed on average.

Of course, some skeptical brand managers will say that these results need to be confirmed and do not apply to their brand. Nevertheless, evidence of the impact effects is accumulating, and the steady progression of exposures to digital, that is, the consumption of (fixed and mobile) Internet media at the expense of other media, means that brands can no longer ignore digital media. The faster they invest, experiment, test, and learn, the faster they will gain a competitive advantage. Other, more academic types of studies are starting to appear and show the impact of digital on sales thanks to the use of advanced econometrics models.[17] More generally, access to "big data" (large, complex data sets) should soon trigger the development of predictive models able to demonstrate the impact of digital on sales and, more globally, the impact of the different components to the marketing mix on sales. We will cover this growing trend in Chapters 7 and 8, which deal with integrated marketing communication and digital marketing dashboards.

The path is marked out, ladies and gentleman of marketing. It is up to you to act, take risks, experiment, and give yourselves the wherewithal to measure the effects of your actions so as to prove their ROI and make further progress.

Key points

1. Over and above clicks and CTRs, digital produces brand effects that it is possible to measure, from the development of awareness through to image, purchase intent, and online and offline sales.

2. Digital multiplies the branding effects of cross-media campaigns and can help to augment awareness, image, and purchase intentions.

3. As well as the direct effects of searches on sales and putting sellers in contact with potential buyers, searches have indirect effects in

terms of branding, and may, among other things, enhance brand awareness and brand image.

 Internet video has effects that greatly increase the impact of campaigns as a result of virality.

Notes

1 For more information and explanation, see www.youtube.com/watch?v=udc-eisEMGU.

2 Kaplan, D. (2013) "Ford expands programmatic video as new TV campaign launches," April 22, www.adexchanger.com/advertiser/ford-expands-programmatic-video-as-new-tv-campaign-launches/.

3 The examples and data are taken from the public breakfast presentation organized on June 8, 2010 by CRM Metrix and P&G France, one of its clients.

4 The results shown are relative and directional in nature. For reasons of confidentiality, we show tendencies rather than give exact figures, but overall these provide an adequate diagnosis. In general, the KPIs are percentages (base 100), which are always compared to norms (in the present case, those of CRM Metrix). These norms allow one to orient the results and put them into perspective compared to other tests carried out in the same context, the same product category, and the same type of brand.

5 For more information, see www.knowledgenetworks.com/dimestore/index.html, or through services available at Dynamic Logic, for example.

6 SmartClip/Nielsen study, 2010, www.smartclip.com.

7 MetrixLab study, 2011, *Advertising Effects Attributes Differentiation and Insights*, www.metrixlab.com.

8 Interview on February 29, 2012. M.-P. Bordet is an associate vice-president of AACC, Association des Agences Conseil en Communication.

9 YouTube Statistics (2011), www.youtube.com/t/press_statistics, December.

10 We return to the metrics and KPIs of virality on YouTube and other platforms in Chapter 6 on the measurement of earned media.

11 We encourage readers to view the ad on www.youtube.com/watch?v=4ba1BqJ4S2M.

12 www.adage.com.

13 De Montigny, M., Utzinger, T., Clement, M. and Shehu, E. (2012) "Why and how ads go viral," *ARF Experiential Learning, Audience Measurement 7.0*. This

paper from MetrixLab outlines a research study dedicated to understanding why and how an ad goes viral. It involved MetrixLab setting up a YouTube channel and combining users' behavioural data with their attitudinal data, derived from a survey that evaluated their attention, memory, ad response, and view of the brand. The results showed that it is vital that the video is watched in full for it to go viral. The study also found that the first seconds and last seconds are the most relevant in encouraging users to share a video.

14 "Demonstrating the branding and engagement value of YouTube advertising," 2009, http://robertoigarza.files.wordpress.com/2008/11/rep-demonstrating-the-branding-and-engagement-youtube-2009.pdf.

15 Panels of consumers whose in-store purchases are tracked and measured and whose media behavior is monitored in terms of TV, press, and online exposure.

16 ComScore (2011) "comScore and dunnhumbyUSA research shows online advertising lifts in-store CPG brand sales," www.comscore.com/Insights/Press_Releases/2011/10/comScore_and_dunnhumbyUSA_Research_Shows_Online_Advertising_Lifts_In-Store_CPG_Brand_Sales, October 11.

17 See, for example, Pauwels, K. and van Ewijk, B. (2012) "Is the classic funnel dead? Sales impact of classic and new online funnels," working paper, May, Aimark Media Efficiency Lab.

chapter 5

Measuring owned media

Executive summary

- Measuring owned media is fundamental because it is the only point of contact that the brand directly controls: it is the center of the brand's digital ecosystem.
- This measurement requires combining quantitative metrics, usually derived from web analytics, and qualitative metrics, through listening to visitors.
- While websites may have different objectives (editorial, commercial, branding, corporate), there are overall transverse measurement systems. Here, even more than for paid or earned media, the decision-maker is able to track dozens of indicators, so it is important to identify those that will enable the right decisions to be made.

Definition of owned media

By definition, owned media refer to all the contact points that the brand or company directly controls. First and foremost, there is its website. Whether it be a brand, corporate, or e-commerce site, this is the only point of contact the brand fully controls. It is true that we could place the brand's Facebook or Google+ page, or Twitter feed, in this category. And the same type of KPIs could be applied to these contact points, but because they are hosted on social networking platforms and not on platforms directly controlled by the brand, we will discuss their measurement in Chapter 6 on earned media. In the meantime, we describe setting up measurements pertaining to the brand website. We recall its central place in the web communication ecosystem and illustrate our remarks by considering the cases of editorial sites, brand sites, and corporate sites.

The website as central to POEM

The results of the 2010 Crop Touchpoint Study, which measured the importance of all the online and offline contact points at each stage of the purchase process (information, purchase, and post-purchase), confirm the omnipresence of word of mouth (Figure 5.1), but also the essential role of the website, both in the search for information and in direct purchasing, in the case of e-commerce sites, and indirect purchasing, for example by encouraging people to go to stores.

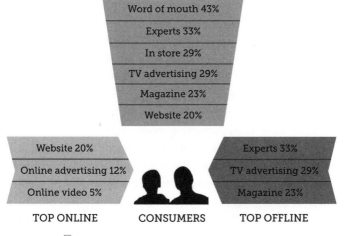

FIGURE 5.1 / The most influential contact points for consumers

Source: Crop.[1]

The above finding is confirmed and largely reinforced by ZenithOptimedia's own findings from its touchpoints database analysis in 46 countries from 2003 to 2012.[2] Among many other interesting findings is the exponential growth of multiple touchpoints available to consumers to interact with brands, and for digital in particular, where the available contact points went up from 9 contacts in 2003 to 36 in 2012. Although not the only digital asset available to brands, the brand website is still in the lead position among the sources of information directly "controlled" by the brand. In 2007,[3] we emphasized the urgent need for brands to "open up" or, in the words of A.G. Lafley, the former CEO of P&G, to "let it go."[4] This observation reflects the necessary change in positioning the brand, going from marketing strategies based mainly on push (through the "paid media" of POEM) to strategies where pull becomes more important. We regularly point out this need for a change of positioning by contrasting brands' constant mono-logue addressed to consumers with their failure to listen to consumers. This lack of listening is especially evidenced by the ratio between investment in market research and investment in advertising and media (www.esomar. org). In 2011, for example, the ratio was 1 to 50, that is, brands spend an average of 50 times as much on talking to consumers than on listening to them. Moreover, such "listening" is relative, since most studies interrogate and question rather than really listen. The market research industry itself is changing (finally), to make way for more collaborative and participatory approaches. Without calling into question the brand's desire for profit, we suggest that improved interactivity would allow it to better satisfy its public and, even more so, establish its legitimacy. In the words of Joseph V. Tripodi, the chief marketing officer of the Coca-Cola Company, brands need to move away from solely "delivering media impressions to generating consumers' expressions," where brand content directly fueled and diffused by consumers themselves becomes the new energy of modern brands.[5] In this sense, the Internet, and more specifically the brand website, is ideally placed to serve these goals. The website is a true marketing hub best able to shape the destiny of brands. Before demonstrating the marketing value of the brand site, we first offer some examples of the use of metrics and quan-titative and qualitative KPIs that can measure and evaluate websites. To do this, we distinguish the cases of editorial, e-commerce, corporate, and, of course, brand sites. To begin, we focus transversally, that is, irrespective of the type of site considered (editorial, e-commerce, brand, corporate), on metrics that allow us to understand the awareness and positioning performance of a website.

Analysis of website SEO performance: metrics and indicators

Search engine optimization (SEO) is defined as the set of techniques for:

> promoting understanding of the theme and content of one or all pages of a website by search engines, in order to make the site visible in a lasting way, capture the traffic using search engines and acquire an image of authority among users. (www.wikipedia.org)

In marketing terms, this is expressed by seeking to develop spontaneous ("top-of-mind") awareness, as well as descriptions – to provide understanding and knowledge of the brand's products and services – on search engines. This task is, of course, essential. In most countries, Google, still the main source for the majority of users for finding information on the Internet, especially its first page of results (two-thirds of search engine users never go any further), puts SEO expenditure between 3 and 5 percent of advertisers' Internet spending.

SEO (apart from the technical aspects of page accessibility by search engine robots that read the content and index it) consists of improving the site's ranking by working on good keywords to include in pages and on tags (headline, meta-description, subheads, summaries, and in paragraphs), in order to mark the multimedia content and name URLs and thus be able to respond to queries made by users when they look for a product or brand. Thus, the key to SEO is the editorial quality of the site – producing unique content (exclusive and on specific topics) that is relevant (to facilitate its retrieval and circulation) and up to date.

In addition, it involves working on the number and quality of the site's incoming links so as to increase its popularity (measured by Google's page rank, or Yahoo!'s and Alexa's backlinks, for example – see below).

Finally, social media, through their dissemination of content, today offer great opportunities to raise the ranking of one's content in search engines.

The metrics used to measure the effectiveness of SEO will be mainly those derived from web analytics. For want of using a particular platform, Google Analytics provides, in its free version, relevant figures that can be used to create KPIs to be put directly into perspective in relation to the overall objective of the site: to sell, inform, enhance one's image. In all cases, the evaluation of performance is implemented over time and is thus tracked in the long term. One must set realistic medium and long-term goals, and give oneself the means to achieve them and especially to measure them in order to progress. Here, we provide some key KPIs for assessing the quality of SEO. These KPIs are constructed from the main quantitative metrics, available through the web analytics data presented in Part 1:

- *Keyword visibility in search engines (rankings):* A basic variable and the most representative of competitive performance. With the growing personalization of search, rankings are increasingly difficult to track and interpret. Nevertheless, if it is placed in a temporal dimension, this KPI is still a good indicator of shortfalls in performance in relation to a benchmark period, and therefore provides an alert for further analysis.
- *The number of different requests at the origin of the traffic:* Apart from keywords, this gives a good indication of the effectiveness of the content in bringing extensive traffic to the site. It reveals exactly which combinations attract people to the site and therefore is of value in thinking about the content of landing pages.
- *Visits by keywords:* Gives another good view of the performance of keywords. Their variation will be interpreted as a decrease or increase in the effectiveness of a particular keyword. In addition, one will seek to maximize the number of keywords used so as to obtain an equivalent number of visits.

- *Visits per landing page:* Provides a measure of the performance of each landing page in terms of natural traffic. In particular, it allows one to measure the performance of each new page on which one wants natural traffic to land: if the indicator does not take off, the question arises as to the good definition/segmentation of the keywords used.
- *Visits per page indexed:* Gives a measurement of overall SEO performance. Each new page indexed cannot automatically provide increased traffic. Nevertheless, one will follow the indicator to see if it falls, which will be proof of the maturity of new pages indexed.
- *Landing pages per page indexed:* Gives a good idea of the proportion of the site likely to attract natural traffic and thus allows its editorial to be corrected and developed over time.
- *Conversions per natural visit:* Gives a clear idea of the business performance of keywords.

Competitive analysis of sites through metrics and KPIs from web analytics[6]

Competitive analysis is an essential component of strategic marketing. However, few sites selling online, for example, are able to clearly define their competitors; their analysis is often based on experience and intuition. Indeed, most analysis from log or traffic data involves optimizing site frequentation: more new visitors, improved conversion rates, analysis of visit routes. Very few analyses use web analytics for purposes of competitive analysis. In what follows we describe the main steps for conducting a competitive analysis of sites. We illustrate the whole process by analyzing the competitive world of two online sales sites: Fnac.fr and Amazon.fr. These two sites compete on the French market selling books, electronic products, and other cultural goods and products. Fnac is the historic leading physical retailer of these types of products in France. In this example, we show that web analytics KPIs can not only help to understand the dynamics of site traffic, but can also identify competitors and market boundaries. Thus they shed new light on competitive analysis.

The study of competition in marketing is based on three key concepts: substitutability, similarity, and the intensity of competition, based on consideration as a whole:

- *Substitutability:* can be defined as being "interchangeable in a particular use situation." It refers the capacity of one brand to substitute for another,[7] and varies according to the use context envisaged by the consumer.
- *Similarity:* by contrast, this is stable from one situation to another. It is based on the comparison of the perception of the characteristics possessed by each product.
- *Measurement of the intensity of competition:* this is based on the overall notion of consideration. In view of limited cognitive abilities and a connective choice process, it is interesting to study the simultaneous consideration of two alternatives (a combined set) by the consumer. Modeling the process of choosing a point of sale can be applied to a large extent to the choice of a site and a distribution channel. This choice goes through several stages: identification of the evoked set of sites on the basis of their perceived characteristics, the process of categorization carried out according to the perceived form, and the cognitive process of multi-attribute evaluation based on the product advantages sought.

Figure 5.2 summarizes the various metrics and KPIs from web analytics for carrying out a competitive analysis of sites.

With regard to conducting a competitive analysis of the Amazon.fr and Fnac.fr sites, we used data from two audience measurement tools available free of charge, provided by Alexa and Google. Alexa functions on the basis of volunteer Internet users, who download the Alexa toolbar. This toolbar allows Alexa to monitor their web browsing and so provides aggregated data for all the websites visited by users; Alexa provides information on 25 million sites (Figure 5.3). Google's various online tools, including Google Trends (which replaces Google Insights) and DoubleClick Ad Planner, work from log data and, like Alexa, provide a relatively comprehensive series of audience indicators (covering both local and global audiences) on numerous sites.

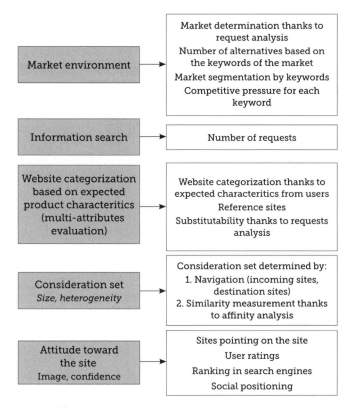

FIGURE 5.2 / **Metrics and KPIs from web analytics available to conduct a competitive analysis of websites**

Web analytics provides information about other sites visited by Internet users. Each query made by a user allows the priority site(s) they consult to be identified, as well as the related keywords. In the case of Fnac (Figure 5.4), the analysis covers three segments: books, technology entertainment products, and arts events. In the books segment, Fnac is in competition with generalists (Amazon, France Loisirs) as well as with actors whose more specialist positioning stands out (Alapage, and queries related to "frequent travellers," "travel"). In the technology product segment, Fnac faces competition from specialists for certain

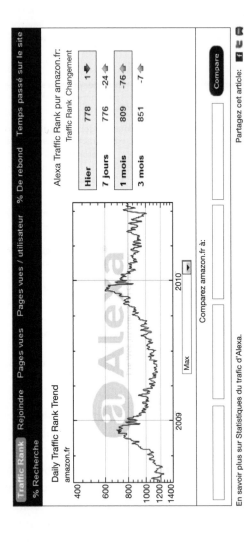

FIGURE 5.3 **Statistics of Amazon.fr traffic**

Source: Alexa, July 2010.

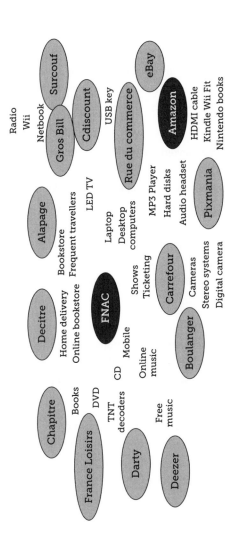

FIGURE 5.4 Representation of the Fnac and Amazon markets through analysis of navigation and queries, July 2010

products (Darty and TNT decoders), discounters (Cdiscount), and innovators with a leading position in certain segments (Amazon and its Kindle). In the arts events segment (as also in laptops), Carrefour is a recognized actor.

The number of requests is an information search indicator and can be measured dynamically by Google Trends. The timeline of requests linked to the different product segments of Amazon and Fnac shows, for example (Figure 5.5):

- An increase in requests linked to television, rising constantly from 2006 to 2010.
- A stagnation, or decrease, of requests linked to books, DVDs, music, and video games, showing a declining interest from 2007 onwards.

This predictive use of Google Trends to estimate allows us to estimate the popularity of certain requests and their history. In the case of Fnac, the site's success is increasingly based on selling multimedia products and not books (July 2010).

Requests bringing the most traffic to the site are identified and used to determine on which product categories each site is most relevant (Figures 5.6 and 5.7). It is then possible to reprocess this information by removing Fnac.com or Fnac requests, with the latter logically representing more than 70 percent of visits.

As shown in Figure 5.6, book queries account for more than 20 percent of the site's traffic. Its popularity (search frequency by users for this keyword) is relatively high, but it is less important than the popularity of Nintendo DS queries, which brings only slightly more than 3 percent of the traffic. With regard to the intensity of competition (number of ads displayed for each query), the keywords "online purchase" and "bridge camera" present the highest advertising pressure.

By analyzing the share of voice, as shown in Figure 5.7, in combination with requests bringing traffic to Fnac website (Figure 5.6), users keying in

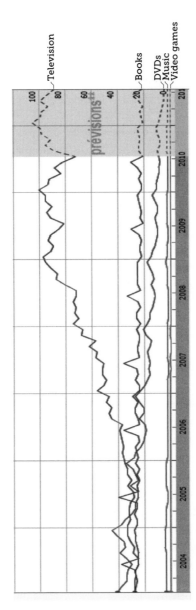

Prévisions = forecasts

FIGURE 5.5 Timeline of number of queries about TVs, books, DVDs, music, and video games

"books" make a purchase in 28 percent of cases at the Fnac site. Fnac retains a strong competitive position for desktop computers, cameras, and stereo systems. It is, however, overtaken on laptops and flat screens by specialists (Boulanger, Rue du Commerce) and hard discounters (Cdiscount). In contrast, Amazon does not appear on these queries, which suggests that the competitive field of the two sites is, in fact, different.

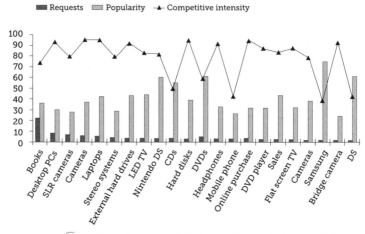

FIGURE 5.6 / Overview of requests bringing traffic to the Fnac website

Amazon has very few queries in common with Fnac when the analysis is carried out on Amazon.fr (Figure 5.8). Analysis of requests for Amazon. com, however, gives a very different picture (Figure 5.9). Books and e-books (Kindle) generate significant traffic to Amazon.com and its affiliate program developed on many partner sites. The domain name is therefore an important factor in the competitive analysis, since in some cases, it refers to product strategies tailored to local markets. In the case of Amazon, the ".com" shows a predominance of technology products like Kindle, whereas the analysis of requests for ".fr" shows a lack of clear positioning, due to the lack of an emblematic product.[8]

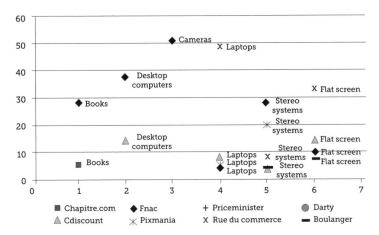

■ Chapitre.com   ◆ Fnac   + Priceminister   ● Darty
△ Cdiscount   ✳ Pixmania   X Rue du commerce ▬ Boulanger

FIGURE 5.7 / Share of voice of different queries by site

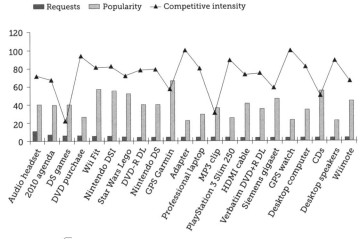

FIGURE 5.8 / Overview of requests bringing traffic to the Amazon.fr site

How to Measure Digital Marketing

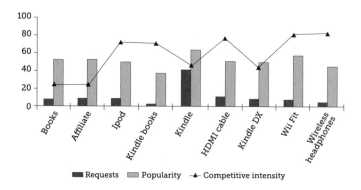

FIGURE 5.9 Overview of requests bringing traffic to the Amazon.com site

Similarity analysis of the sites (in July 2010) through affinity[9] confirms that Amazon.fr and Fnac.fr are not really in competition. Other sites have more direct affinity with both of them. In our example, it emerges that the sites having greatest affinity with Fnac.fr are Surcouf.com and Chapitre.com (Figure 5.10); those having greatest affinity with Amazon. fr are Alapage, Webdistrib and Pricerunner (Figure 5.11). Here, there are a number of sites that have been identified in Figure 5.7.

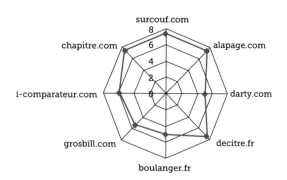

FIGURE 5.10 Main sites with affinity to Fnac.fr

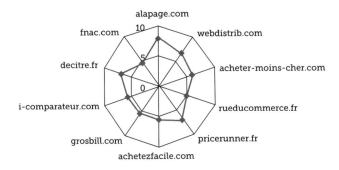

FIGURE 5.11 Main sites with affinity to Amazon.fr

Even though, strictly speaking, the use of metrics and KPIs from web analytics presented here is not, at first sight, intended to measure the effectiveness of digital marketing, analysis reveals the utility of such indicators for the purpose of measuring the frontiers of the markets of sites, and therefore their positioning. We recommend that site managers also use them for these strategic purposes. We now return more specifically to the use of metrics and KPIs useful for site evaluation, beginning with editorial sites.

Measuring and evaluating editorial sites

Editorial sites live and grow according to the quality of content they put online. It is content quality that will enlarge the audience, and increase its loyalty and the time it spends on the site. This model typically concerns portals – such as Yahoo.com or press and TV sites – which are at once brand sites and content sites and which have to find the right balance between information available offline and online. This business model also applies to many professional and individual websites, which sometimes aim to make available specific content for visitors seeking such information. The beauty of the web lies in its capacity to bring together people who are passionate about or at least interested in the same things. To illustrate the use of quantitative and qualitative KPIs for measuring and evaluating this type of site, we turn to Marc Fray, our former CRM Metrix colleague and an expert in digital marketing, who is also fascinated by the city of Berlin. We thank Marc for kindly sharing his passion and expertise in explaining how he uses various indicators to advance his site, www.berlin-en-ligne.com.

History of the site www.berlin-en-ligne.com

Marc Fray, who has a great interest in history, first went to Berlin in 1992, three years after the fall of the Wall. He was charmed by the city and has subsequently always kept abreast of its news. Up to 2000, Berlin was not adequately presented on the French-language web. At that time, even German sites offered very little content in French. In March 2000, Marc Fray launched his website with a view to counteracting the prevailing image of Berlin as a sad and ugly town, an image no doubt inherited from its past. He wanted to present another Berlin, told through its history, architecture and heritage.

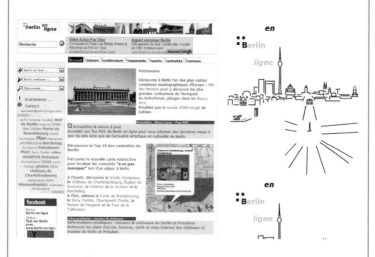

FIGURE 5.12 Old homepage of www.berlin-en-ligne.com

Source: www.berlin-en-ligne.com.

> At the outset, with only 25 pages of content, the site was submitted to Yahoo! France. Registration of www.berlin-en-ligne.com in the directory in July 2000 was the first launch of the site on the web. Voilà, Excite, AltaVista, AlltheWeb, and Google immediately ranked www.berlin-en-ligne.com among the top five sites on Berlin.

Inventory of existing data for measuring the site's performance

The data sources used include:

- Google: to determine the site's "competitive position"
- Google Analytics: to identify quantitative changes in the audience
- Incoming emails and the site's satisfaction barometer: to obtain qualitative feedback from visitors.

With reference to the AIDA model, the available metrics more or less perfectly cover each stage of the model:

- *Attention:* as a pure player site, awareness of www.berlin-en-ligne.com is based entirely on SEO.
- *Interest:* it makes sense to make the use of the available indicators from web analytics, for example bounce rates, number of pages per visit, time spent on site.
- *Desire and action:* comes down to a reduced number of indicators from web analytics, which refine and complement the qualitative analysis of emails sent and satisfaction feedback provided by the visitors' exit survey.

Table 5.1 summarizes the main KPIs used. Interpretation of the KPIs sheds considerable light on the site's digital performance.

TABLE 5.1 KPI used to evaluate the performance of Berlin-en-ligne.com in relation to the main stages of the AIDA model

Stage of the AIDA model	Google	Web analytics	Satisfaction barometer emails received
Attention/ awareness	Present in the top three Google search results for the keywords in relation to the signature: "Guide pratique, touristique et culturel, de Berlin et Potsdam"	Number of unique visitors	Participation rate in the satisfaction questionnaire Number of emails sent
Interest/ quality of experience	Number of external referrals to www.berlin-en-ligne.com	Average time spent Number of pages per visit Bounce rate	Understanding the subject matter of the site www.berlin-en-ligne.com Satisfaction score
Desire/ commitment		Percentage of repeat visitors	Measurement of positive vs. negative comments Recommendation score
Action/ intention		www.berlin-en-ligne.com RSS feed click rates	Partnership proposal Cross link request Recommendation score

Monitoring the strengths and performance of SEO

Daily monitoring of queries about Berlin in Google gives an indication of the positioning and nature of the competitive field. On Google, www.berlin-en-ligne.com lies behind an "encyclopedia" entry, namely Wikipedia, and ahead of a practical entry, that of the Berlin tourist office (www.visitberlin.de).

Editorial is the key to a successful SEO. As well as regular updating of content, compliance with the rules of web writing and linking has contributed to the consolidation of the site's page rank and keeping www.berlin-en-ligne.com among the top five search results on Berlin (Figure 5.13).

Statistics from AT Internet, which specializes in online web traffic measurement, show a steady growth in the number of visitors and visits from 2000 to 2008 to www.berlin-en-ligne.com, with a peak in 2009 on the occasion of the 20th anniversary of the fall of the Berlin Wall. While the number of page views has been broadly stable since 2003, the number of page views/visits and visit duration has been falling gradually since 2002 (Figure 5.14).

Images

Maps

Vidéos

Actualités

Shopping

Blogs

Plus

Paris
Changer le lieu

Le Web
Pages en français
Pays : France
Pages en langue
  étrangère traduites

Date indifférente
Moins d'une heure
Moins de 24 heures
Moins de 3 jours
Moins d'une semaine
Moins d'un mois
Moins d'un an
Période personnalisée

Tous les résultats
Sites avec des images

Plus d'outils

Berlin - Wikipédia
fr.wikipedia.org/wiki/Berlin
Berlin est la capitale et la plus grande ville d'Allemagne. Située dans le nord-est du pays, elle forme un land (État fédéré) à part entière et compte environ 3,4 ...
↳ Histoire de Berlin - Mur de Berlin - Porte de Brandebourg - Berliner Ensemble

Berlin Allemagne maps.google.fr

Berlin en ligne - Introduction - Guide pratique, touristique et culturel ...
www.berlin-en-ligne.com/
Guide pratique, touristique, et culturel. Visite virtuelle des monuments, musées et curiosités de **Berlin** et Potsdam.
 Vous avez partagé ce résultat.

Berlin en ligne - Accueil - Guide pratique, touristique et culturel de ...
www.berlin-en-ligne.com/home.htm
Accueil **Berlin** en ligne : Guide pratique, touristique et culturel de **Berlin** et Potsdam - Présentation du patrimoine, actualités, mises à jours, fils rss, top 10 des ...
 Vous avez partagé ce résultat.

Berlin – portail touristique officiel pour les visiteurs de la capitale ...
visitberlin.de/fr
Berlin Tourist Information: des hôtels, des billets de spectacle, des offres forfaitaires ainsi que des informations importantes sur l'offre touristique pour votre visite ...
↳ Berlin Tourist Information - Découvrir - WelcomeCard - Voir

Berlin - Offizielles Stadtportal der Hauptstadt Deutschlands - **Berlin**.de
www.berlin.de/ - Traduire cette page
Stadtportal **Berlin**: Offizielle Informationen des Landes **Berlin**, der Landesregierung und nachgeordneter Bezirke und Behörden sowie wichtige Informationen für ...

A **Berlin**. Un guide de **Berlin** et un Blog

FIGURE 5.13 Monitoring of KPIs from web analytics: an up-and-down progression

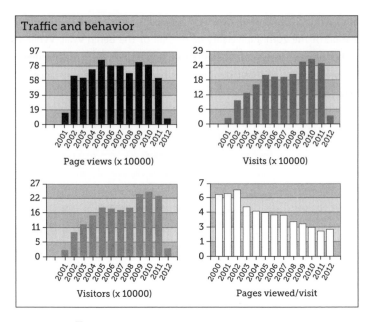

FIGURE 5.14 Analysis of website visits

Analysis of emails sent by visitors

The growth of traffic observed by AT Internet was also accompanied by an upsurge in emails from visitors asking for documentation (metro map, maps, brochures of Berlin). It seems that visitors to www.berlin-en-ligne. com were mistaking it for the city hall site or the Berlin tourist office site. Was this a symptom of a discrepancy between the desired position and the positioning perceived by visitors?

Message received on 12/2/2012

Hello, I would like to get hold of documentation on the Berlin Congress Center, and on specific theaters such as the Berliner Ensemble, the Berlin Philharmonic, the Deutsche Opera, and so on.

Thank you in advance

Valérie

Diagnosis

- Growth then stabilization of the number of unique visitors.
- Fall in average visit time and number of page views per visit.
- Increasing number of visitor emails apparently intended for the Berlin tourist office.

Hypothesis

Is the fall in the average length of visit and number of page views/visits indicative of the reduced capacity of www.berlin-en-ligne.com to meet visitors' expectations?

The qualitative contribution of attitudinal KPIs

To confirm or disconfirm the hypothesis, a satisfaction barometer for the site was set up in late 2007, with a view to determining:

- the profile of visitors
- reasons for the visit
- the quality of the experience.

Since 2008, 5,848 questionnaires have been collected, with 70 percent of respondents completing the questionnaire (Figure 5.15).

Analysis of the SiteCRM (a standardized continuous analysis of marketing and business impact of websites provided by MetrixLab) results reveals a portal with varied visitor profiles and expectations:

- A diversity of age groups – 33% are aged under 25, 33% are aged 25–54, and 34% are 55 and over.

- 47% of visitors are preparing for a stay in Berlin, 33% of visitors are interested in cultural activities, while 15% are schoolchildren, students, and teachers.
- 75% are first-time visitors to the site, the same figure as provided by Google Analytics.

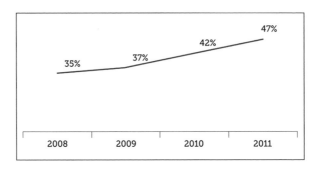

FIGURE 5.15 Percentage of travellers wishing to arrange a stay in Berlin

The proportion of undertargeted visitors in the audience tends to change with time, with more visitors to www.berlin-en-ligne.com seeking practical information. This trend seems to slightly impact the bounce rate and visitor satisfaction (Figure 5.16).

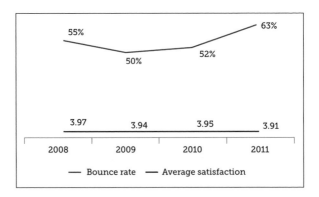

FIGURE 5.16 Change in the bounce rate and average satisfaction

Analysis of the number of page views per visit according to the keyword entered in search engines confirms the diagnosis (Table 5.2). The number of page views per visit is generally lower for keywords in the practical register: map (in French: *plan* or *carte*), transport, youth hostel.

TABLE 5.2 Analysis of number of page views per visit

Keyword entered in search engine	Visits	Pages per visit	Average time spent on site
Berlin	13,545	5.75	00:04:09
Map of Berlin	5,086	2.89	00:03:07
Map Berlin	4,218	2.61	00:02:41
Museum Berlin	2,174	3.43	00:03:11
Berlin youth hostel	1,826	1.38	00:01:34
Map Berlin	1,296	2.27	00:02:14
Berlin map	1,194	2.58	00:02:47
Map of Berlin	1,176	2.83	00:02:35
Museum Berlin	982	3.71	00:03:06
Visit Berlin	981	6.19	00:03:53
Museum of Berlin	933	2.94	00:02:53
Berlin museum	872	3.55	00:03:24
Berlin transport	748	1.6	00:01:34
Berlin museums	685	4.35	00:04:23

All in all, www.berlin-en-ligne.com visitors come to the site with objectives that tend not to lead them to discover the full extent of the site.

Lessons for action

The joint interpretation of behavioral and attitudinal KPIs guided the drafting of specifications for the redesign of the site www.berlin-en-ligne. com. Its main principle was based on a rebalancing of the architecture between cultural information and practical services. Although the content concerning history, architecture, and monuments is still available, it will no longer be the main entry key to the new version of the site, both in terms of navigation and the zoning of the homepage. The future range of practical services should aid visiting related pages.

Key conclusion

Capitalize on the quality of the editorial content, respond better to the expectations of visitors actively preparing trips to Berlin, and renew opportunities to revisit the site through RSS feeds and other digital touchpoints (Facebook, Twitter, Flickr).

FIGURE 5.17 New homepage of www.berlin-en-ligne.com

Source: www.berlin-en-ligne.com.

Measuring and evaluating brand sites

Mass marketing usually gives pride of place to so-called "volume strate-gies," where the goal is to "sell as many products as possible to the largest possible number of consumers." The result is a media strategy where a huge number of contacts is generally preferred, to the detriment of the quality of contacts in the targets reached. Although this strategy might have been effective, it is becoming less and less so. Indeed, today, all media professionals agree that media effectiveness is becoming increas-ingly costly. The classical models of media planning are reaching their limits, with a high risk of consumer saturation. Conversely, consumers are looking for closer contacts with the brands and companies they are interested in. Rather than *frequent* media, we can say today that people *consume* media. They do not hesitate to directly contact brands with which they wish to maintain and develop a more personal relationship. There are many ways to do this, including call centers, the Internet, and brand websites in particular. In all these cases, it is no longer the brand that seeks to contact the individual, but the consumer who comes to the brand. Therefore, such contact can no longer be evaluated simply in terms of number or quantity, but above all should be evaluated in terms of quality. It is not surprising that brand sites are high value touchpoints, since on average 85 percent of brand site visitors are customers or pros-pects with a strong affinity for the brand or the product categories where the brand is present.[10]

The site is an exceptional point of convergence, which attracts the best customers for a brand, namely those who spend the most (20/80 law), as well as consumers who are opinion leaders, since they tend to be overrepresented on brand sites by a factor of three to four.[11] In Chapter 3, we gave the example of the Omo brand site, www.omo.fr, which, in order to promote itself, needs to go beyond purely quantitative indicators, derived from web analytics (such as the number of unique visitors, the average time spent on site, and the bounce rate), and "defend" the value of a few thousand visitors to the site, when other media, such as television, allow the brand to instantly reach huge numbers of prospects and customers. The point is that the brand website can reach and attract a higher value target. The quality of contacts, as measured by qualitative KPIs, enables a site – in this instance a French mass market brand – and its central role in the brand's digital ecosystem to be measured and better valorized (Figure 5.18).

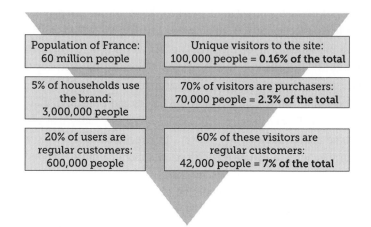

Population of France: 60 million people	Unique visitors to the site: 100,000 people = **0.16% of the total**
5% of households use the brand: 3,000,000 people	70% of visitors are purchasers: 70,000 people = **2.3% of the total**
20% of users are regular customers: 600,000 people	60% of these visitors are regular customers: 42,000 people = **7% of the total**

FIGURE 5.18 / **The brand site, a way of getting in touch with the brand's best customers**

Source: SiteCRM database.

Visits to the brand site have a significant impact on purchase intention, attitude toward the brand, and in-store purchasing behavior. To investigate this, a control sample of visitors – for which measurement of purchase intent is made at the start of the visit – is compared to a test sample – for which the measurement is made on exiting the site (we should make it clear that these two samples are made up of first-time visitors to the site). Over the whole SiteCRM database, the increase in purchase intent following the visit is around 5 percent. Moreover, the positive effect of the visit on declared purchase intent doubles through a positive effect on brand affinity, that is, presence in the consideration set;[12] when the visit is considered satisfactory, the visitor favorably alters their degree of affinity with the brand.

That said, this average increase masks wide disparities. While the increase may reach 60 percent for some sites, there may also be isolated negative impacts, when the experience of the site is viewed very unfavorably. The positive experience of the site allows a significant increase in purchase intent and affinity (Tables 5.3 and 5.4).

TABLE 5.3 Purchase intent before/after visiting the site

	Measurement of purchase intent on entering the site	Measurement of purchase intent on leaving the site
Very unlikely	0.6%	0.5%
Unlikely	1.0%	0.9%
Neutral	13.9%	6.2%
Probable	24.9%	17.1%
Very probable	59.6%	75.2%

Note: Chi-square test significant at $p < 0.001$.

TABLE 5.4 Brand affinity before/after visiting the site

	Affinity with the brand	
	Measurement of affinity on entering the site	Measurement of affinity on leaving the site
Low	17.5%	7.0%
Medium	60.5%	61.7%
High	22.0%	31.4%

Note: Chi-square test significant at $p < 0.001$.

Further analysis shows that the impact is stronger for less well-known brands. While the average impact of visiting the site on purchase intent is around 5%, it is 5–7% for lesser known brands (against 2–3% for the best known brands). This differential impact is also reflected in the affinity score with the brand.

More than 15 years' experience measuring mass market and consumer goods brand sites shows that these results are directly correlated to actual purchasing behavior and purchasing frequency. Many brands, such as Coca-Cola, Danone, L'Oréal, and so on, confirm that Kantar consumer panels (for example) illustrate the findings in terms of sales, both for brand sites and relational program sites.

Auchan: a French international retail group

A recent study for Auchan also reveals the strong correlation between variations in visits to Auchan.fr and in-store sales. The analysis[13] shows that an increase in the number of visitors to the Auchan.fr website is generally predictive of higher sales in Auchan stores (Figure 5.19).

More specifically, the detailed results show that in the period from January 2007 to July 2009, for LCD TVs, up to 13% of sales are directly attributable to the Auchan.fr site, whereas only 3% of sales are made directly online.

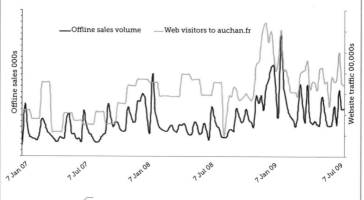

FIGURE 5.19 Correlation between the number of visitors to Auchan. fr and sales in Auchan stores

---

At a time when many advertisers are looking to expand the digital presence of their brand, these results more than ever militate in favor of the central role played by the brand site. This observation is even more true today. With brand pages on Facebook not fully under the control of the brands concerned,[14] the brand website is the only point of digital contact that the brand truly owns and controls, and on which it can orchestrate the relationship it wishes to implement and maintain with its various publics. As we have already said, but it bears repetition: *the brand site is a real brand marketing hub, a central point for push and pull marketing.*

Apart from commercial performance criteria – purchase intent, affinity, and in-store purchasing – is visiting a site likely to influence attitude toward the brand? Indeed, if brands today are incarnated in very different ways – products, packaging, advertising, contact personnel – the total brand experience is based in part on the experience of the site. A bad experience can have negative consequences on the perception of the brand, while a good experience will result in a positive perception.

On this point, data from the SiteCRM database shows that the more the online experience is viewed positively by users, the more their attitude toward the brand improves (Table 5.5). Nearly 50 percent of visitors who are very satisfied with their experience on the site say that they favorably revise their attitude toward the brand. This finding applies equally to regular visitors.

TABLE 5.5 Relationship between the level of satisfaction with the visit experience and attitude toward the brand for first-time visitors

		Satisfaction regarding the visit experience				
		Very dissatisfied	Dissatisfied	Neutral	Satisfied	Very satisfied
Change of attitude toward the brand	Very unfavorable	26.3%	2.1%	0.3%	0.1 %	0.1 %
	Unfavorable	22.8%	16.8%	1.1%	0.5%	0.1%
	Neutral	40.3%	72.8%	77.3%	60.3%	47.7%
	Favorable	4.9%	6.5%	16.8%	28.5%	17.5%
	Very favorable	5.7%	1.8%	4.4%	10.6%	34.6%

Note: Chi-square test significant at $p < 0.001$.

In the end, accumulated experience and the results of studies show that the "natural" touchpoint, that is, the brand website (which people come to freely instead of the forced exposure imposed on them by traditional media), is a key point of convergence, where, at any time, interested or curious consumers can come to obtain information, learn more about the brand, engage in exchanges, or become more involved in their relationship with the brand. Whether this happens spontaneously or because of a TV advertisement, information on packaging, an online or offline promotional operation, or a personal recommendation, the brand site is, in our opinion, a contact point that potentially offers exceptional ROI. It is up to advertisers to make it a central component of their communications ecosystem.

EXPERT VIEWPOINT

Guillaume Weill
Managing director, CRM Metrix Europe

Do you think companies have fully appreciated the importance of their website in their communication strategy?

At CRM Metrix, we have been measuring and evaluating the impact of brand, corporate, e-commerce, and editorial websites since 2000. The exponential growth of our business in all sectors attests that an increasing number of companies and brands measure, more than simply count, their visits and visitors. However, the road is still long and there are many opportunities. Around the world, on average nearly 50 percent of visitors to a site still do not find what they are looking for.

Are social networks the new El Dorado for brands?

It is true that social networks attract more and more consumers and hence brands. After their Facebook page, brands set up their Google+ page. But all too often, this is done at the expense of digital managers paying attention to their various brand websites. This can be a fatal mistake, because the site is and will remain the only point of contact that the brand or company fully controls. Our measurements show that its effectiveness has not diminished over the past 10 years. The future of brands depends very much on the right articulation of paid, owned and earned media.

Measuring and evaluating corporate sites

A truism that is nevertheless too often neglected in the case of corporate websites (where the number of visitors is often only a few thousand) is that the number of visitors alone says little or nothing about the effectiveness of the site. Indeed, the results of the e-corporate barometer database show that visitors to a corporate site are very varied, so it is essential to identify them in order to serve them better. Every site manager should describe the site's audience, so as to bring the visitor effective added value in accordance with their profile and needs. Current and potential customers account for about 20% of visitors. This result shows the importance of thinking about "customers" on corporate sites, as well as thinking about "investors." This trend is widely present today on the websites of publicly quoted companies. It has been shown that the number of "investor" visitors amounts to only about 10% of the total, a finding that underlines the importance of not overloading corporate sites with financial information, which is sometimes largely inaccessible to many visitors. Corporate sites are also a source of information for the company's collaborators (12%) (employees and business partners) and job seekers (9%).

Figure 5.20 shows that the four main targets of a corporate website can be defined according to the visitors' profile and their reasons for the visit (the advantages sought):

- Customers looking for information on products/services
- Job seekers looking for information on training courses and job offers
- Employees looking for social information
- Shareholders looking for social and financial information.

As with brand sites and editorial sites, satisfaction with corporate websites has a significant and strong relationship with opinions about the company (Table 5.6).

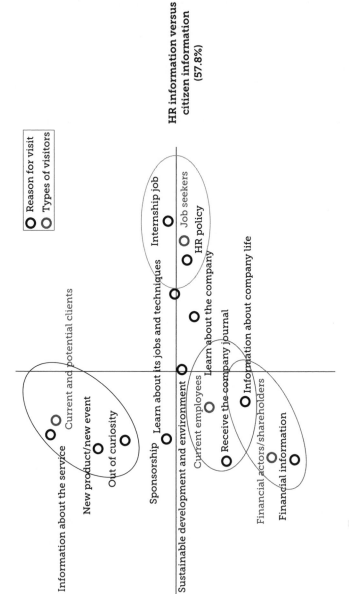

FIGURE 5.20 Reasons for the four main targets' visit to corporate sites

TABLE 5.6 Relationship between satisfaction and opinion regarding the company after visiting the corporate website

| | | Change of opinion regarding the company | | | | |
| | | After visiting the site, your opinion of company X is | | | | |
		Considerably less favorable	Rather less favorable	Unchanged	Rather better	Considerably better	Total
Overall satisfaction	Very dissatisfied	117	132	199	10	2	460 (4.9%)
	Fairly dissatisfied	18	105	452	38	3	616 (6.5%)
	Neither satisfied nor dissatisfied	9	75	1,272	219	28	1,603 (17%)
	Fairly satisfied	7	23	3,182	1,335	204	4,751 (50.3%)
	Very satisfied	4	4	1,020	519	459	2,006 (21.3%)
	Total	155 (1.6%)	339 (3.6%)	6,125 (64.9%)	2,121 (22.5%)	696 (7.4%)	9,436 (100%)

The results show, among other things, that among all satisfied visitors (fairly satisfied and very satisfied), 37% have a better opinion on the company at the end of their visit to the corporate website (rather better opinion and considerably better opinion). This percentage is similar for customers and job seekers: 38% of customers and 36% of job seekers who are satisfied with their visits have a better opinion of the company. It is lower for financial actors and current employees as only 29% of financial actors and 24% of current employees satisfied with their visits have a better opinion of the company.

Ultimately, even though indicators from web analytics provide information on the progress of the attention paid by the different audiences to the company (number of visits, number of visitors), these solely quantitative metrics are insufficient for evaluating the site. Logically, they must be complemented by more qualitative indicators, such as those provided by the e-corporate barometer. It is up to corporate communications managers and their web teams to develop measures capable of guiding the effectiveness of their actions. Everything depends on getting the right balance between quantitative and qualitative indicators.

Having reviewed and explained the various tools and means available for measuring and evaluating the impact of websites, in Chapter 6 we turn to the measurement of earned media.

Key points

1. The website is a strategic asset at the center of the brand's digital ecosystem and its "POEM" strategy.

2. Web analytics provides many useful metrics for carrying out a competitive analysis of the site and optimizing performance at each stage of the AIDA model, but those quantitative KPIs need to be complemented by more qualitative metrics to provide a full perspective on website ROI.

3. The type of site – editorial, brand, corporate, or e-commerce – guides the selection of the most appropriate web analytics KPIs. Qualitative KPIs are largely complementary to those from pure web analytics and should be able to respond to the optimization requirements of each type of site, for example by evaluating the quality of visitors to a brand or corporate website, or by precisely identifying the motivations for the visit or the reasons for neglecting an e-commerce site.

Notes

1   *The Crop Touchpoints Study – Mastering the Communication Mix*, www. crop.ca/sondages/pdf/2010/Touchpoint_article01.pdf. This is a North American study; Crop handled the Canadian portion, while their New York-based partner CRM Metrix handled the US portion.
2   Database of touchpoints studies run by the Zenith Optimedia network, worldwide. Reported at IREP Conference, Paris, March 2013.

3   Florès, L. (2007) "When consumers come to the brand," *Brands Review*, July, www.prodimarques.com/documents/gratuit/59/quand-le-consommateur-vient-a-la-marque.php.

4   Opening address at the annual conference of the Association of National Advertisers, October 2006.

5   Tripodi, J. (2011) "Coca-Cola marketing shifts from impressions to expressions," HBR Blog, April 27.

6   Comments and examples come from an academic research project led by Professors Maria Mercanti Guerin (CNAM) and Laurent Florès (INSEEC).

7   Perceived product substitutability has an evaluative character and is based on the concept of preferences or the evoked set. Substitutability can be operationalized, according to the preference level (intensity of attitude) or the evoked set.

8   Kindle was underdeveloped in the French market (July 2010). However, given the prominence of the Kindle sold at cost in France for Christmas 2011 and since, it is likely that analysis of these periods will give different and interesting results.

9   Affinity is calculated using the same method as practiced in media planning, namely the relation expressed as a percentage or as an index between the target audience and the total audience of a medium, program or time slot. In the case of the Internet, the base is the population of users.

10 These results are provided by the CRM Metrix SiteCRM database, which currently contains more than 100 million observations.

11 Vernette, E. and Florès, L. (2004) "Communicating with marketing opinion leaders: How and in which media?," *Decisions Marketing*, 35: 23–37.

12 Brand affinity is measured as follows: Which of the following sentences best describes your relationship with brand X? High affinity corresponds to the answer: It is the only brand of detergent I buy, while average affinity is: X is one of the two or three detergent brands that I buy regularly. The other five positions on the scale are aggregated to represent a low affinity.

13 IREP Effectiveness Seminar, March 2010, Analysing the effectiveness of the marketing mix, Pascale Carle (Auchan) and Peter Chain (MarketShare).

14 Facebook Timeline controls exposure of the content posted by brands so that only a portion of the people listed on the page are actually exposed to it. Posts made by brands are therefore not seen by everyone signed up to the brand page, but only by some of them.

chapter 6

Measuring earned media

Executive summary

- Measuring earned media is a matter of some complexity, linked to their inherent nature, which blends both spontaneous actions and/or reactions, as well as the diversity of social platforms.
- Measurement needs to be based on consumers and their usage of the media concerned: it is about who spontaneously transmits messages about the brand to their audience or whom the brand asks to transmit messages to.
- The measurement systems make use of various tools (web analytics, tracking systems, textual analysis, surveys), but human intervention is essential for properly analyzing the conversations.
- There are a number of metrics, often "proxies" rather than genuine measurements.

Earned media: a new El Dorado to be understood and measured

If 2010 was the year in which social media took off from the standpoint of their uses, 2011 was the year in which advertisers became aware that

such uses had become inescapable for developing effective digital marketing directed at their consumers. Far from being isolated channels within
which people discussed topics that interested them, over the course of
just a few years, social networking sites have acquired a key position in
the uses of the Internet. Real audience crossroads, major information
relays, and initiators of the new uses of the web, they are profoundly
changing advertisers' digital ecosystem – and this is only the beginning.

Today, these social media are the prime vectors of what is called "earned
media," that is, everything that allows a brand to improve its presence on
the Internet outside its own contact points and without resorting to buying
space of any kind. Although their importance is increasingly incontestable,
it is still difficult to understand the weight they have in terms of investment
in the digital marketing mix, as their inherent nature makes their evaluation
complex. How can one distinguish what concerns the efforts deployed and
what concerns the users themselves and their propensity to share and pass
on information? All of this makes measuring them a specific exercise.

Nevertheless, according to a recent study by Forrester,[1] it appears that
the proportion of web investment devoted to social media is 26 percent –
supported as a whole by meteoric growth in just five years. For this
reason, understanding better how to measure their effectiveness has
become a major issue for digital marketers: the much discussed "ROI" of
social media is on everybody's lips today.

This chapter aims to take stock, up to the present, of a topic which, even more
than the points addressed in the measurement of owned and paid media, is
a work in progress, subject to the emergence of new platforms, which lead to
new uses by their users and new possibilities for advertisers to exploit.

> Pinterest is a photo-sharing service, based on the idea of
> the cork board, where one pins up photos. When we started
> writing this book, it was still in its infancy. But nine months
> later, the traffic it generates on the largest US websites
> is greater than that of Google+, LinkedIn and YouTube
> combined, according to the website mashable.com.

Thus, to explore this topic, it is important to first take stock of the objectives that can be assigned to the use of earned media. Accordingly, we review the main features of the tools, their uses by consumers, and their significance for brands. Second, we specify what measurement objectives may stem from the use of earned media, by referring to the AIDA model. Finally, we discuss the metrics to be used, the tools needed to measure them, and the key indicators to be constructed, monitored, and analyzed when one wishes to account for the effectiveness of earned media. As you will see, unlike other chapters, the relatively "fluid" character of earned media led us to more fully define the platforms and their uses. We have tried, therefore, to envisage their appropriation by brands, within the framework of the AIDA model, and to define the types of metrics and KPIs that can measure the effects at each stage of the model.

What are the objectives for a presence in earned media?

Earned media and social media constitute a world that is far from stable, both in terms of platforms and their uses. Consequently, taking account of them in the digital marketing mix requires shedding light on and understanding a number of important features, allowing us to work on an "all other things being equal" basis, and to set up a useful and operable system for measuring effectiveness:

- It is important to understand the *usage logic* underlying their adoption and not focus on the latest fashionable tool. Indeed, what became of all the investments made in the virtual world Second Life, or the initiatives taken, particularly by those in the music industry, in relation to the Myspace platform? Needless to say, at all costs you must be present on a medium that is growing in order to benefit from a windfall effect; if you do not think about your presence and interactions in terms of what users want to see, hear, and share, specifically on the social web, you will certainly go astray.
- *Setting out without goals is worse than not setting out at all*. As Benjamin Franklin said, when asked about his time management: "Failing

to plan is planning to fail." This maxim is particularly true for earned media. Unlike a paid-for web campaign, which, if it fails, will soon be forgotten (or will not even have been seen at all), or a brand site on which you always have time to make changes, opening a channel for dialog with the brand's stakeholders, through a presence in the earned media, is involving and irreversible: the more consumers anticipate entering into direct communication with the brand, the more they will be disappointed and dissatisfied if that promise is not kept.

- Even more than with owned and paid media, *every strategy or operation*, and therefore every system for measuring its effectiveness, *should be focused on individuals*. With earned media, consumers are ready and willing to be or become bearers of the messages the brand wants to transmit. It is necessary to build everything around them and their needs, hence the importance, as we shall see, of listening processes.

- As a corollary to the preceding point, remember that for earned media, it is not always the brand that is the source of the stimulus whose effectiveness one wishes to measure: *much of the content and behavior* that one wants to measure is *spontaneous and stems from individual initiatives*. If one does not know who is speaking, to whom they are speaking, and why they are speaking, measurement of effectiveness will be incomplete.

- The *temporal dimension* is crucial here, insofar as the expected effects of certain efforts occur over a time period of variable length. Thus, considering earned media within a perspective of understanding, measurement, and management – in relation to its e-reputation, for example – may not be a short-term exercise.

Finally, it must be noted that with earned media, the situation of sending and receiving messages is very different from that pertaining in more traditional advertising and marketing. Nevertheless, we must not forget that the latter are there to serve objectives that are themselves traditional, objectives we have described extensively through the AIDA model.

Consequently, the process of measuring the effectiveness of earned media involves using and creating specific KPIs and being in a position to make the link between platforms and heterogeneous new usages, on the one hand, and tangible marketing objectives shared by all the company's decision-makers, on the other: the subject of the operationality and understanding of metrics is, as we shall see, one of the major challenges in establishing an effective measurement system for earned media.

Earned media: what are the tools and uses for consumers and brands?

Many advertisers are uneasy with the myriad social tools used today by consumers, and, like them, you might be tempted to limit the presence and actions of a brand in these social media to the opening of a fan page on Facebook and the community management that ensues from it. That would be to misrecognize and misunderstand the web's social ecosystem and the various opportunities it offers brands that want to profit from it today.

Here, we outline the different social spaces of the web in order to specify their major uses and see how brands can mobilize them within a marketing perspective.

Consumer opinion forums and platforms

Although currently consumer opinion forums and platforms seem to be less in vogue than social tools that allow users to manage their social networks and exchange all types of messages (text, videos, images), it should not be forgotten that forums and, more precisely, their predecessors bulletin boards gave rise to the web's social function – they began in the early 1980s, before the html protocol came into general use – and remain one of the richest sources in terms of interactions on the social web.

One thinks here of the large public forums, such as craigslist or Usenet, where every day hundreds of thousands of people discuss a huge range of subjects, depending on their areas of interest. Similarly, one also thinks of consumer opinion sites, where consumers, especially in the area of travel and tourism (for example TripAdvisor), share their opinions about destinations, accommodation, and so on.

Here, we are in the realm of spontaneous exchanges and we can easily categorize what is said in these forums and platforms according to what motivates the writer:

- Complaining, expressing satisfaction, or sharing a negative/positive *experience* in relation to a brand.
- Expressing a positive or negative *opinion* about a brand without it being connected to an immediate experience.
- *Asking for advice* about a product, service or brand.
- *Giving advice* about a product, service or brand.

Air France carefully tracks and analyzes discussions that take place in the international forum flyertalk.com. This is now the richest source on the web for understanding how the high-value customer segment – frequent flyer passengers who travel by air at least three times a year for professional reasons – behaves and reacts (Figure 6.1). It has nearly 400,000 active members.

FIGURE 6.1 Home page of flyertalk.com forums

Source: flyertalk.com.

Similar to these venues are the commentary threads about articles published in online media, which can also be sources of rich discussions, even if they more naturally focus on major topics and policies than advertisers' marketing topics. In this respect, taking them into account will be interesting from the perspective of corporate communications, public relations (PR), and public affairs.

From a marketing perspective, in relation to forums, it will be worthwhile for a brand to listen to and analyze the conversations that take place, and categorize the speakers, the context in which the discussions arise, and their extent and content. In such situations, listening is most often passive, since activating communities as an advertiser needs to be done carefully, with a real desire for transparency and exchange, otherwise there is a risk of interrupting the dynamics and being rejected. Consequently, using ambassadors who are themselves already reference points in the community seems more appropriate.

Blogs

Although there are currently nearly 180 million blogs worldwide (www. Alexa.com), the attention they receive from advertisers is less today than in the period 2006–07 – the celebrated Web 2.0 era – and especially before the sensational arrival of Facebook in the public sphere. In addition, a dual tendency is making itself felt in the world of blogs: on the one hand, the professionalization of the most popular of them, whose status thus shifts from that of "notebooks" to quasi-media, and, on the other, the inactivity of the great majority of them, which form a "long tail," to the advantage of social platforms; for example, among the thousands of blogs on the Skyrock platform, we see a considerable decline in terms of activity.

By definition, a *blog* is a place for the creation and dissemination of information on one or more specific topics, in the form of *posts*. This particular form calls for genuine writing and editing work – if we exclude spam blogs or "splogs" produced for advertising purposes, the aim of which is to create virtual traffic to increase websites' search engine optimization performance, using the technique known as "black hat SEO," against which search engines struggle. Blogs are, in fact, limited to certain types of users, with the ability to produce, over a long period of time, writing similar to journalism; for example, while more than a third of French people use Facebook daily, it is estimated that fewer than 1 percent regularly write and maintain a blog.

This fact also accounts for the success of microblogging platforms such as Twitter or more recently Tumblr, which are based on the principle of sharing files and images/videos/texts and their accompanying microblogs, or microposts.

Consequently, a brand may consider the use of blogs in two ways:

- Producing a blog itself so as to generate content related to its business, with a view to sharing it with customers and prospects. It will then be situated within an owned media strategy.
- Addressing the ecosystem of blogs pertaining to its market and its environment, either by listening so as to track the opinions of experts and those they have exchanges with (posts), or by directly acting on the blogger community, through operations that will most often be for the purposes of PR or influence/public affairs.

Facebook

Facebook is the platform that launched the real social use of the web. We will not dwell here on how it works for users (sharing news, photos, and everything one likes on the web and beyond), or on its power and central role in the web ecosystem. Nevertheless, it is important to distinguish the three types of roles it can play for an advertiser:

- *Owned media:* Setting up and maintaining a fan page for the diffusion of messages.
- *Paid media:* Use of the platform as a web communication medium in absolute terms, or for bringing traffic to one's fan page or one or more sites.

• *Earned media:* Monitoring and analyzing conversations that take place on the platform, either on the fan page or more generally through public conversations.

Twitter

Opened to the public in July 2006, Twitter's original concept was to allow updates to be shared with one's friends via SMS – in fact the service was first developed to meet the flow and availability management needs of a taxi company.

Progressively gaining traction as it became mediatized, particularly through major news events, Twitter currently has well over 500 million accounts worldwide (517 million as of July 1, 2012), including more than 140 million in the USA alone (Figure 6.2). User base growth is slowing in Japan and South Korea, yet Japan is still one of the most active countries. In June 2012, the top three cities by number of tweets were Jakarta, Tokyo, and London.[2]

However, these figures need to be taken with a pinch of salt, by distinguishing between the number of accounts activated and the number of actual users, because a good many accounts are simply robots automatically generating statuses and information and many "human" accounts are inactive. Indeed, global statistics usually show that about 60 percent of Twitter accounts are not used regularly. Nevertheless, if we are interested in Twitter's real uses and their typology, in the context of a marketing operation, the following practices can be isolated:

• *Diffusing web information* of which one is the source: journalists, PR professionals, brands.
  Passing on web information according to one's interests (retweets): bloggers and consumers more generally.
• Making a complaint, expressing satisfaction, and *sharing a positive or negative experience*, as for forums, but in a more condensed format, with greater sharing potential.

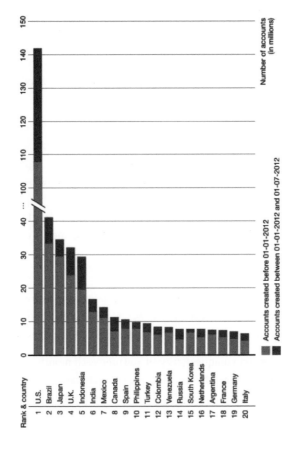

FIGURE 6.2 Top 20 countries in terms of Twitter accounts

Source: Semiocast, © 2012.[2]

- Expressing a positive or negative *opinion* about a brand, without it being associated with an immediate experience, but most often in response to a news item; for example, the mechanism of live tweeting (commenting live on Twitter), which has become central on the network during major events – TV broadcasts, high-profile news, conferences and events, concerts, and cultural events.
- *Asking for or giving advice* about a product, service or brand is less frequent, because the community is not theme focused and people do not necessarily seek expert opinion there.

In view of these uses, a brand may approach Twitter from a marketing perspective so as to listen to and, via its thread, host appropriate conversations, but also – and this is the characteristic significance of Twitter users – to intervene and interact during conversations with a much lower risk of being rejected – subject to using it appropriately and with a genuine readiness to engage in dialog, as Twitter users are particularly sensitive to overly aggressive advertising messages or PR.

Video platforms: YouTube, Dailymotion, Vimeo

With the advent of high-speed and, before long, ultra high-speed Internet access, video is the most obvious way for web users to share items of interest. The figures[3] below indicate the scale of the phenomenon:

- Over 800 million unique users visit YouTube each month
- Over 4 billion hours of video are watched each month on YouTube
- 72 hours of video are uploaded to YouTube every minute
- 70 percent of YouTube traffic comes from outside the USA
- YouTube is located in 53 countries and across 61 languages
- In 2011, YouTube had more than 1 trillion views or around 140 views for every person on earth.

It is easy to understand advertisers' interest in investing in such networks from an earned media standpoint, that is, going beyond the advertising dimension and intervening in platforms and videos, in order to capitalize on users' propensity to view, share, and comment on videos posted by brands. Advertisers may also be interested in videos posted by users about the brand, but it is essential to be careful about their purpose, the nature of the issuer, and their content.

Photo-sharing platforms: Picasa, Flickr, Instagram, Pinterest

Along with the use of video, photo sharing has become a huge phenomenon on the Internet, first on the basis of private or semi-public hosting platforms supported by major search engines (Google with Picasa, Yahoo with Flickr), but subsequently, and in a more social and viral way, with the development of tools such as Instagram (the sharing of stylized photos taken with a mobile phone) or Pinterest (sharing images depicted as pinned onto cork board). Here, it is the rapid growth of the mobile Internet and the use of smartphones that underlies the logic of appropriation by the general public. Brands can use these platforms by being the source of conversations, by creating, publishing, and updating pages and threads, and by tracking the reactions that these give rise to.

> Some major brands make use of corporate pages on LinkedIn to promote their products. In particular, HP has used this approach in the USA to publicize its products among company decision-makers.[4] This has resulted in:
>
> - more than 2,000 recommendations by professionals in the network close to those who follow the brand
> - more than 20,000 new registered members on the brand page
> - nearly 50,000 updates shared on the network about HP and its products.

With greater difficulty, they can try to monitor the spontaneous photographic production that concerns them. Indeed, proper tracking of such content depends on users being able to clearly mark photos with titles or tags, since automatic recognition is not yet possible at present.

Other platforms: LinkedIn, Quora, Path

There are also many other platforms offering uses of varying degrees of development – bookmark sharing, web page sharing, profile management, professional network management, advanced question/answer platforms, multimedia sharing of the day's events – and connecting with communities of varying degrees of openness – connections are selected according to specific criteria, for example professional or expertise based. Here again, their appropriate use for marketing or communication purposes will depend on the final objectives pursued by the brand, from simple presence or passive listening through to deeper engagement with a community or communities.

E X P E R T V I E W P O I N T

Jan Rezab
CEO and co-founder, Socialbakers

Your company offers metrics and analytics to help brands monitor and measure their social media presence on a variety platforms. Can you tell us what measurement purpose you primarily serve?

There are several needs we help to solve, based on our clients' feedback. We help them:

- Analyze a variety of platforms and social media profiles to improve their performance
- Better understand their competitors
- Report on customer service
- Benchmark competitors.

Although metrics and KPI may vary per social media platform, what are the key concepts you want brands to pay attention to?

Social media marketing has shifted from only looking at fans to looking at different ways of engaging customers. Today, these metrics are engagement, reach, and customer service metrics like response rate. In the future, I believe social media metrics will evolve into understanding things like engagement loyalty (are my fans from last year still engaging with me today?), and many other things.

To your knowledge, is there one magic bullet KPI that could measure the whole value of social media ROI?

I don't think there is magic bullet, it all depends on different platforms and verticals. If you are an airline, your KPI other than awareness of locations will be customer service and direct ROI. If you are a telecom company, your primary objective other than crisis management situations will be to raise awareness of certain activities going on and at the same time customer care. If you are a chocolate company – that's a whole other story – its all about reach and engagement. From my point of view, there is no magic bullet.

What are the measurement objectives for earned media presence?

The world of earned and social media is complex, and brands that want to invest in them can do so in various ways, with heterogeneous audiences and for their own specific reasons, depending on the membership communities and platforms used. However, by looking at platforms and their characteristics, we can identify some major constants in the objectives pertaining to their use, which will allow us to categorize these objectives according to the stages of the AIDA model and thus to define specific indicators for measuring the effectiveness of earned media.

Attention objectives

Attention objectives cover all the efforts made by a brand to attract the attention of audiences and consumers. Measuring this attention can be done by means of the indicators of awareness and knowledge of the brand and its products.

With regard to earned media, we have seen that, whatever the tool or platform used, a brand will seek to initiate and engage consumers in conversations and/or measure and analyze existing conversations. Here, we are in the area of what has long been called (and still is for some professionals) "buzz marketing" or viral marketing, the characteristic "word of mouth" of the Internet and social networks.

When we talk about viral marketing, we are referring to marketing techniques that use the practices of social and earned media – as well as other common practices, such as social SEO, which involves using social media to increase the chances of being seen by search engines – to develop and raise brand awareness and increase mentions of the brand in the communities one wants to reach. Thus, measurement will tend to be quantitative in nature and, if one is the source of the stimulus, to simply count the number of times it is viewed/read and/or its evolution over time:

- the number of views of a YouTube video or Instagram photo
- the number of times a blog post is read
- the number of times a post on a Facebook page is seen/reached
- the number of earned media results on the first X pages of the results of a search engine search
- the proportion of inbound links from social media in a website's traffic – and evaluation of these compared to their equivalent in terms of buying advertising space or one's search engine marketing budget.

In addition – and this applies to cases where a marketer is in a listening position and wants to estimate the amount of feedback from existing tracking of a brand in earned media – a marketer can also, as we pointed out when describing the various consumer metrics, endeavor to track the number of mentions or occurrences of the brand and/or its products and/or the stimulus it has introduced. In relation to such measurement, three main principles are important in its implementation:

1 *The existence of a fixed reference point:* Measuring and tracking the number of mentions over time cannot be done if the reference system is constantly changing. For this reason, it is better to have a panel-type approach and a sampling method within this, so as to obtain an "all other things being equal" measurement.

  For example, we could envisage working on listening to a finite number of areas of conversations and/or individuals, such as an influential blog panel, or a constant sample of brand followers on Twitter. Then, within this panel, a marketer will endeavor to count the number of occurrences of the brand and its products specifically and its competitors more generally, or, if the reference system is too large and/or the techniques for identifying the mentions is too complicated to be used on a large amount of text, randomly sample a limited number of conversations.

2 *Capacity to "disambiguate" terms:* Since it is a matter of counting the number of mentions of brands or products, again we must be sure that we know what people are talking about, easy enough if it's called Häagen-Dazs Cappuccino Caramel Truffle but rather more complex if it's called Orange (a telecom company).

3 *Capacity to describe the speakers:* The marketing techniques applied to earned media call for an in-depth knowledge of the areas we want to activate and the people whose discourse we wish to measure and describe, or indeed address.

This involves working on understanding the sources we want to insert into the panel. Like any quantitative measurement of opinion, buzz needs to consider what is said according to specific criteria describing the person speaking. These criteria are the components of what some people call – wrongly or through a misuse of language, taking the term from its common usage in PR and media analysis – influence. It is pretty clear that someone with 50 Facebook friends who mentions your brand will have less influence than someone who does so in a community of 5,000 friends.

Interest objectives

When it comes to an earned media marketing strategy, arousing the interest of consumers by focusing on the advantages and benefits of one's brand and its producers, as well as demonstrating those advantages, calls for an initial level of engagement on the part of these consumers. Appealing to consumers by sending a stimulus or noting how they talk about the brand is not enough. Instead, it is a matter of starting a conversation with them. Here again, measurement will be largely quantitative.

The first idea of quantitative interest for the brand and what it does in earned media is measured by counting the simplest interactions the individual may have with it or one of its stimuli. As well as views and reads, and taking account of the three principles above, the number of "likes" on a Facebook post, the number of "I like/I do not like" on YouTube, or the number of retweets of a piece of information on Twitter will be tracked. Although such interactions do not prove a high level of engagement, they do reveal greater engagement toward the message from the brand or a member of the network.

Furthermore, once a brand has invested in its own point of social contact, the people who follow the efforts made by that brand must also be counted. Thus, the followers of the brand will be counted, whether it is the number of fans on Facebook, the number of followers on Twitter, or the number of views for a video. Although it is the simplest measure, it clearly indicates whether what has been produced by the brand or about the brand (user-generated content) manages to attract a specific public.

On the basis of these two main types of measurement, simple metrics of the engagement level can be defined.

Desire objectives

Here, it is a matter of measuring higher conviction or engagement levels toward the brand and its products. We move on from the "slight" inter-action levels discussed above and focus on stronger interaction, which involves engaging consumers in discussion and exchanges. It is always important to bear in mind that in social media, the 90-9-1 rule generally applies: 90% of people do no more than glance at what's happening, 9% interact with the content created by other people, and 1% are genuine creators of content.

This rule provides a theoretical framework that a recent Forrester survey has been trying to quantify more accurately,[5] by questioning tens of thousands of people about their behavior on social media. Users are classified into six groups, according to their degree of participation.

These six groups, which are not completely exclusive because interactions are taken into account, are as follows:

1 *Creators* publish a blog, produce their own web page, write articles, or publish videos of music they have created.
2 *Conversationalists* update their status on a social networking site, post updates on Twitter.
3 *Critics* post opinions on community platforms and forums, and comment on articles or blog posts.
4 *Collectors* aggregate RSS content, make a note of videos, or tag photos.
5 *Joiners* use Facebook and/or Twitter solely for personal reasons.
6 *Spectators* read/view content on blogs, forums, and video or opinion platforms.
7 *Inactives* have no social interaction.

Figure 6.3 below shows the findings of this survey for the USA and Europe.

Admittedly, we are far from a theoretical 90-9-1, but we cannot fail to see that there are few real producers of content and that, in Europe in general compared to the USA, there are more "inactive" consumers. From the standpoint of the brand with an earned media strategy, being able to measure and analyze what the 9 percent and the 1 percent do and say requires taking account of the exchanges and behavior of those consumers who are most involved and willing to enter a dialog with the brand.

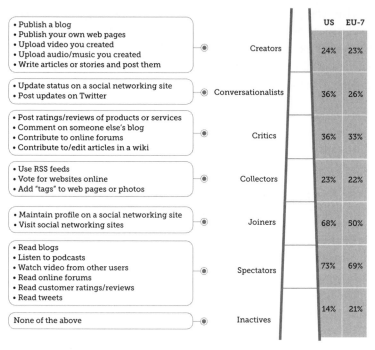

	US	EU-7
Creators	24%	23%
Conversationalists	36%	26%
Critics	36%	33%
Collectors	23%	22%
Joiners	68%	50%
Spectators	73%	69%
Inactives	14%	21%

Creators
• Publish a blog
• Publish your own web pages
• Upload video you created
• Upload audio/music you created
• Write articles or stories and post them

Conversationalists
• Update status on a social networking site
• Post updates on Twitter

Critics
• Post ratings/reviews of products or services
• Comment on someone else's blog
• Contribute to online forums
• Contribute to/edit articles in a wiki

Collectors
• Use RSS feeds
• Vote for websites online
• Add "tags" to web pages or photos

Joiners
• Maintain profile on a social networking site
• Visit social networking sites

Spectators
• Read blogs
• Listen to podcasts
• Watch video from other users
• Read online forums
• Read customer ratings/reviews
• Read tweets

Inactives
• None of the above

Note: Base: 57,924 US online adults (18+); 16,473 European online adults (18+)

FIGURE 6.3 Six groups of users of social media, percentages for USA and Europe

Source: North American Technographics® Online Benchmark Survey, Q3 2011 (US, Canada); European Technographics Online Benchmark Survey, Q3 2011.

More than the volume of information produced – number of responses to a blog post or to a Facebook status, number of interactions following a forum post or a tweet, number of comments on an online press article or YouTube video – we are interested in the content of these comments and interactions. Here, it will be a matter of isolating and attributing the content, while being sure that the discussion or message really concerns the brand or its products, as well as describing it in terms of conversation themes (uses, brand image), tonality (questions of monitoring and analyzing sentiment, which we describe later), and the speaker's capacity to be read, believed, and repeated (measuring influence, which we also describe in more detail below).

Action objectives

This final set of objectives concerns anything that measures the propensity of consumers to engage in purchase or conversion action online or offline, following or in parallel with their involvement in earned media in relation to the brand and its products. It goes without saying that these are the most important objectives for any type of online or offline communication, because it is through them that we can begin to develop a true calculation of ROI.

As Olivier Blanchard – author of the key book *Social Media ROI*[6] and known on Twitter under the pseudonym @thebrandbuilder – explains, if a brand makes a dollar investment, it is in dollars that it should measure the return on investment. Figure 6.4 illustrates this point.

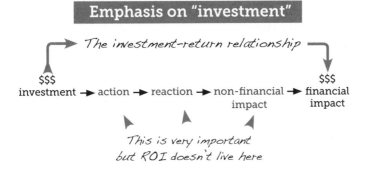

FIGURE 6.4 Approach to calculating the ROI of social media

Source: Blanchard.[6]

Clearly, the intermediate objectives of the AIDA model are important, but ideally the final measurement of the impact of earned media actions, in terms of sales and/or propensity to buy, is required for a real view of ROI.

Measurement of the final stage of the AIDA model from a consumer point of view will be done mainly by questioning consumers on their purchase, for example. We previously illustrated such an approach in the case of paid media, with the example of the Oral B campaign in Chapter 4.

One can also evaluate from the digital contact points where conversion is possible (a website or fan page offering an e-commerce functionality) the specific weight of purchasers who have come by way of earned media or who are members of the brand community. Here, we are close to an analysis of the effectiveness of owned media and will always wonder about the anteriority of the different contact points in the decision-making process.

Metrics and KPIs for the measurement of earned media

First, let us recall the four main principles for correctly implementing a measurement of earned media:

1 *User-centric measurement:* We are interested in individuals and their behavior (and not just their behavior, as is the case of web analytics behavioral measurements for owned media), which requires being able to describe them and knowing where and how they express themselves.
2 *A measurement framework:* With regard to a measurement within a fast-growing environment, it is important to work within a fixed framework and/or be able to correct the measurement bias related to the natural increase in the populations visiting the platform; for example, is getting 1,000 brand mentions on Twitter at T1 and 2,000 at T2 due to the brand being more in people's minds or to a larger number of users?
3 *Measurement of spontaneous and reactive behaviour:* It will have to be capable of measuring spontaneous behavior on the part of consumers, but also behavior solicited through various stimuli (campaigns, videos).

4 *Quantitative and qualitative measurement:* A special effort should be made with regard to the construction of indicators, especially when trying to translate a spontaneous textual utterance, which is therefore qualitative, into quantitative indicators.

This complexity of measurement will require a simplification of metrics, in order to bring them into analytical frameworks and effectiveness measurement that can be understood and adapted, with regard to the objectives that brand managers have set. For example, if the aim of a Facebook page is to engage in conversations with the brand's prospects so as to make them want to try it, focusing solely on the number of fans or the potential reach of a message will be insufficient.

Attention objectives: giving meaning to counting

It is advisable here both to quantify simple actions through web analytics-type metrics (the number of views and reads) and to be able to count the number of mentions of a brand and/or it products. Thus, we can use standard web analytics tools, taking care to tag each piece of content posted on the social media, for tracking these metrics.

Key metrics

The number of times a blog post is read, the number of messages in a forum thread, the number of views for a video, the number of people potentially reached by a tweet or impressions (the sum of all the followers of my followers: the TweetReach tool can track, for a given hashtag, its number of mentions and the people who have contributed most to its visibility within the Twitter community), and the number of people potentially reached by a Facebook status or "friends of fans" in the Facebook Insights dashboard.

Regarding the second objective, measurement will be done through a monitoring tool or social media monitoring, enabling you to count, as

exhaustively as possible, the mentions of a brand or its products, on various social platforms. There are a large number of tools, ranging from those that are free of charge through to solutions costing several thousand euros per month, offering analytical services, human support, and integration of human flows in the business processes of the company.

Free tools

- Google Alerts for all the mentions visible through the search engine
- Blog Pulse, Technorati, Icerocket, blog platform specialists
- Hootsuite, TweetDeck, Seesmic, for Twitter and Facebook
- BackType for comments
- Omgili for forums.

Paid tools

Radian6, Sysomos, Lithium, Alterian, Crimson, Visible Technologies, Brandwatch, Synthesio.

Here, we are concerned not with exploring these solutions and their functionalities, but with how they should be used to fulfill this counting objective.

The three pillars of a good monitoring strategy for identifying and counting the mentions of a brand or its products (and therefore of the tool and the indicators it will provide) are:

1 *The right definition of the scope of the sources to track:* This involves control of platforms where consumers can express themselves, which in turn is based on good knowledge of the natural ecosystem around the brand and its problematics, for example TripAdvisor if one works in tourism, but also on the use of crawlers that will openly inspect, through search engines or other indexation systems, parts of the social web, in order to find out about new sources of expression; for example, insurance forums, where people can talk about travel compensation and therefore link up with brands active in tourism.

The relevance of incorporating certain source typologies should also be considered: not all brands are able to generate videos or obtain online press articles that give rise to comments.

Once this detection process is complete, a panel of stable sources needs to be set up, within which measurement can be implemented, since the principle of crawling allows the detection of sources whose relevance will be confirmed each time by incorporating them into the panel.

2 *The right description of sources:* To be able to assign a weight to the mentions that are discovered, it is important to evaluate some type of "echo potential." This involves using a number of indicators, such as Google's Page Rank checker, the number of unique visitors for blogs, the number of friends, fans or followers for Facebook and Twitter, or the number of contributors for forums. In the absence of a common denominator, try and assign a score to each of the sources of your panel to take account of its capacity to be seen, read, or followed.

> **Be careful**
>
> These platforms should not be viewed as sources in their own right: they host users, each of which is a source. Treating them as a whole in accordance with the principle "one person, one voice" would be a methodological mistake.

3 *Correctly identifying product names and disambiguating them:* Since it is a matter of mentions of brands/products, there is no problem when these are objectively monosemic and Internet users clearly refer to them by their names (for example Nikon D4). But it becomes more complicated and requires considering a set of associated terms for brands with various (mis)spellings or slang names (for example (McDonald's, MacDonald's, Maccy D's) or when the names themselves are ambiguous (Orange, Carrefour).

It will then be necessary to look at the content, first to make sure that it really concerns the brand and second that the mention is relevant.

> "I'm leaving McDonald's" is a nonrelevant mention of the brand, whereas "I'm leaving McDonald's and the service was very good" is a relevant mention.

Finally, since brands will often be used in a discussion context, we also need to ask about the capacity of the tools to note the mentions in discussions at various levels (like forums), without necessarily being able to identify semantic markers (reference to the brand or its products). Indeed, in a conversation about a brand, it is unusual for the participants to repeat its name every time they speak.

> Original message: "I'm leaving McDonald's and the service was very good."
>
> Reply: "Yes, it was, wasn't it."
>
> This reply should be counted as a further relevant mention of the brand, even though it is not explicitly named.
>
> **Key metrics**
>
> The number of mentions as a gross total or weighted over a period, the brand's share of voice in the mentions (in the context of monitoring several brands), changes in the number of mentions over a media coverage period, the number of mentions centered on a specific advertising initiative, for example a TV campaign, and the number of mentions specific to a platform if this is specifically activated.

Composite indicators can also be defined across two measured attention dimensions:

- *Level of centrality of discussions:* The total number of mentions compared to the total number of messages in a forum. This can determine to what extent the brand is central to the discussion.
- *"Audience" equivalence:* The number of mentions multiplied by the number of people potentially reached (impressions), an indicator similar to advertising value equivalency, used in PR to quantify the effects, by multiplying the number and size of effects obtained by the audience evaluation of the media in which they were obtained.

Interest objectives: quantifying the first levels of engagement

As regards measuring interest in earned media, we have mentioned two parallel kinds of quantitative measurement:

- Counting the number of people who are "engaged" in relation to spontaneously shared content or content the brand wishes to share (number of fans, number of followers).
- Counting the basic interactions on the various platforms, such as retweets, ratings in opinion platforms, +1 from Google.

These two concepts are closely related and will, in the future, become increasingly important for web marketers, in order to define true indicators of performance and effectiveness. With regard to the first dimension, the figures are easy to find in platforms and analytics tools.

Key metrics

Number of Facebook fans, number of Twitter followers, number of members of a forum or unique visitors to a blog, and number of members of a YouTube channel.

With regard to the second dimension, although the past five years have been marked by the race to critical mass (fans, followers), decision-makers are beginning to understand that without engagement or dialog, it is difficult to ensure real earned media presence and relevance. Social media are essentially based on dialog and exchange. In fact, failing to encourage consumers to participate, share, question, and reply is to risk seeing them go elsewhere and interact with competitors, or else complain.

To take the example of Facebook, the need to engage fans and more generally users is becoming a major concern for brands. Indeed, we are reaching the point where it is crucial for brands to position themselves in the Facebook world, where the best of them will be able to take real advantage of this tool. The coming years will see Facebook maturity for everyone, and maturity in marketing and communications means ROI.

First, we think of maturity on the part of users, who, if they now "like" around five brands on average, more than 50 percent have already "unliked" a page.[7] For pages, this is reflected by the rate of engagement (see below) that barely exceeds 2 percent (in this regard, the tool and site socialbakers.com offer an interesting compilation of statistics on the main brand pages). This figure is still worthwhile in the world of the web, where click-through rates are falling from year to year, but may be disappointing for brands that want to maintain a regular dialog with a real fan base.

Furthermore – and this is something that brands may learn to their cost – in opening a two-way communication channel, the brand cannot then go into reverse. It necessitates a presence and constant investment, at the risk of being subject to criticism and seeing the entire strategy called into question.

Finally, the most striking point, Facebook is currently making key strategic moves to become a reference platform in terms of paid media, and therefore intends to monetize everything that brands have been able to create up until now without payment to the platform. The first indications of the network's strategy, which were glimpsed at its annual conference on 8 September, 2011, have since been confirmed:

- Renewed focus on the user and social functions through the implementation of the new timeline.

- More possibilities for filtering and highlighting certain information with EdgeRank, a randomization algorithm to determine what should be displayed in users' news feeds, which increasingly prioritizes high interaction content.
- Open Graph, which allows more lightweight interactions with applications.
- A more comprehensive detailing of history on the network.

All this means even more reduced visibility for brands on their fans' walls. In this regard, in July 2011, the PageLever tool revealed that fewer than 10 percent of fans were likely to see a brand status posted on their wall, and this figure decreases with the number of fans of the brand.[8]

We find ourselves in a situation where users can quickly abandon their relationship with the brand if it does not talk to them, where brands are anxious to maintain satisfactory traffic, visibility, and engagement, and where the network is tending to decrease the natural visibility of brands, thus driving them to win and create loyalty in ever more traffic.

The result is a cost per click for ads that increased more than 50 percent in the last quarter of 2011, initiating a movement already familiar on Google and the traditional display networks – the higher acquisition costs for useful traffic. For brands, it seems as though the golden age of the spontaneous community, committed and (almost) free, is over.

Without being alarmist, it seems obvious that all the social platforms, in search of viable economic models, are joining this move to monetize their audience base. Therefore, we attach great importance to the measurement of interest in relation to earned media.

Key metrics

Number of likes, comments, shares, and other interactions (cf. new interactions made possible by Open Graph), following a Facebook status; number of retweets of a tweet;

number of +1 for Google+; number of responses to a blog post; and number of comments on an online press article.

These metrics are of interest in terms of their absolute value, but especially in terms of their relative temporal and competitive value.

The composite indicator across the two interest dimensions measured will be the rate of engagement, which is defined at time T as the ratio between the number of interactions and the number of people potentially reached by the earned media initiative carried. Facebook, for example, has already started to integrate this concept through the "People talking about" metric, which aggregates, for a given page, all actions initiated by users, such as the fact of posting on the page, commenting, sharing a post or content on the page, answering a question put to fans, and mentioning the page.

EXPERT VIEWPOINT

Michael Scissions
CEO, Syncapse

Your company offers platform and enterprise management systems to help brands monitor and measure their social media presence on a variety platforms. What measurement purpose do you primarily serve?

We enable marketers to understand and maximize investments across paid, owned, and earned social media. Social data have created an unprecedented opportunity to move from campaign-based mass marketing to always-on hyper-segment marketing. We dive deep into a brand's social connections so we can identify the most important audience segments and what content and message frequency resonates best with them. We call this social audience relationship management, and we apply this framework to the complete marketing cycle, including planning, execution, and measurement/attribution.

Although metrics and KPIs may vary per social media platform, what are the key concepts you want brands to pay attention to?

We believe social performance happens when marketers achieve balance across four key pillars:

1 Targeting and understanding
2 Paid social media
3 Brand stories and content
4 Community management and support.

This approach enables a better understanding of a brand's social state, and identifies strengths and capability gaps. It also enables data-driven examples and scorecards that incentivize best practices and higher performance within large marketing organizations.

To your knowledge, is there one magic bullet KPI that could measure the whole value of social media ROI?

There is no single "magic bullet" KPI that measures the whole value of social media ROI. The reason is that every marketer and every brand has different KPIs. The key is to standardize social metrics and map them to your own internal KPIs, and adopt scorecards that become brand operating principles. While there is no magic bullet, all brands can understand and improve their social and overall marketing performance by applying simple, yet rigorous measurement frameworks.

Desire objectives: analyzing content, and its tonality and impact

It is with regard to these desire objectives – whose measurement should reflect the propensity of individuals to persuade/be persuaded by an earned media stimulus in relation to the brand and products – that we will need to fundamentally address their expression, and therefore their meaning, and not merely the quantitative manifestations of these stimuli.

Consequently, these objectives draw on many concepts with regard to measurement: classification of sentiment, tonality, e-reputation, and influence. All these "catch-all" words conceal as many measurement results, which we now attempt to decipher.

Classification

Once we have isolated the conversations about brands and products, the most difficult step will be to give a basic description of them. The first task is thematize the content. Do not forget that we are dealing with spontaneous expressions and that the same message may therefore come under several themes or categories.

First, all content that is of no interest and/or purely factual should be removed. Each content will then be arranged thematically, so as to structure the relevant information within a monitoring plan. As with a questionnaire or a survey interview guide, a monitoring plan must be constructed, which provides a comprehensible information structure for consultation, transmission to third parties, and retrieval for analytical purposes, since one will definitely be able to randomly retrieve messages in sufficient volume for the sake of economy. This monitoring plan allows the categorization of information on multiple themes and subthemes, either defined when setting up the project or subsequently identified.

To describe this information, text mining software can be used, which deploys logical information classification scenarios, defined in advance by the team responsible for the monitoring project. After this, human a posteriori validation is carried out, to ensure the quality of the automated text mining classification.

In an e-reputation monitoring project carried out for the Air France group, no less than 16 themes (from the most corporate-oriented to the most product-oriented, via HR and risk themes) and nearly 180 subthemes were used to thematize the discourses monitored on the Internet.

Key metrics

Evocation and share of voice of different expression themes and subthemes.

Sentiment and tonality

In a first step, the general meaning of the information must be described. Thus, for each categorized and relevant piece of information, the overall tone or sentiment must be defined. This is done using semantic analysis software, which gives a first level and first orientation of tonality. Subsequently, human intervention is required to manage the subtleties of language, syntax, and registers of expression (doubt, irony), and to understand the contexts.

Automated techniques for analyzing sentiment, and more generally the automated processing of language, are the "hired help" of monitoring problematics, the objective of which is to track reputation.

Although useful for risk detection and the analysis of large volumes of information (they are widely used in the fields of insurance and intelligence), these techniques have not yet demonstrated their relevance with respect to marketing or advertising projects. Indeed, in addition to providing trend indications, software such Luxid from Temis or that provided by Arisem-Thales is still too expensive to be used for such projects. Their implementation requires large investment upstream, in terms of intelligence software and database construction, dictionaries, and systems of reference. In addition, they have trouble analyzing unstructured and nonlinear language, which is characteristic of

conversations on the Internet, although they are much more relevant for the processing of journalistic language.

Finally, only humans can move to the next step, which involves entering into a qualitative stage to dissect, reduce, and classify statements, bring them into line with knowledge of the context and objectives of the measurement project, and put them into perspective in accordance with speakers' personal and collective dynamics, beliefs, and values. This goes beyond the simple stage of describing tonality, since a post/comment/message is inherently multivocal. Semantic software becomes a support for human analysis.

To capture sentiment and tonality, a five- or six-point metric scale is used:

- *Extremely positive:* the speaker is very positive about the theme and uses highly favorable vocabulary.
- *Positive:* the speaker is positive about the theme and uses empathetic vocabulary.
- *Neutral:* no clear position about the theme.
- *Ambivalent:* the speaker balances the pros and cons around the theme without adopting a final standpoint.
- *Negative:* the speaker is negative about the theme and uses pejorative vocabulary.
- *Extremely negative:* the speaker is very negative and uses vocabulary that discredits, rejects, or strongly criticizes the theme.

Key metrics

Overall sentiment toward the brand, sentiment by theme and subtheme, share of positive sentiment among all mentions, and share of voice of brands in positive sentiments in a market.

On this subject, we note the approach used by the network Razorfish, which has developed a simple model – social influence marketing (SIM) score – constructed in the same way as the net promoter score of the brand, with the following two formulas:

Net sentiment = (positive mentions + neutral mentions – negative mentions)/all mentions

SIM score = net brand sentiment/net industry sentiment

E-reputation and influence

It is still surprising to find that some people think that the reputation of a brand on the Internet can be put into an equation, as for a brand equity model. This mistake must be avoided, given the diversity of possible measures of earned media, whereas the measurement of brand equity may happen through market surveys that provide a homogeneous source of metrics. It is especially presumptuous concerning the ability of the equation to match the value of a Google SEO classification with the number of positive mentions on Facebook or a net negative sentiment in forums. In short, a magic formula for e-reputation, as you will have realized, does not exist.

The same goes for influence. The concept appeared with the rise of social networks, since the capacity to promote or criticize goes hand in hand with the capacity to exert influence on other people. This very PR view of the issues of information circulation on the Internet is today largely discredited. Admittedly, some bloggers have managed to unite audiences and, as such, are likely to influence the purchase decisions of those people who read them. And consumers all say that the recommendations of their peers have a strong impact of their purchase decision. Nonetheless, it is the case that the measurement of influence cannot be reduced to the simple fact of being potentially listened to, or having an audience. Moreover, without taking into account the relevance and tonality of the discourse and the criticality of the subject for the brand, it is difficult to say whether the messages sent or relayed by a community have an influence, and who in this community is particularly influential.

This is why we provide a simple analytic framework for calculating influence.

On the social web, an opinion ecosystem is based on places of influence, constituted by sources; these places are inhabited by isolated individuals or by people joined together by ideological, professional, personal, or social affinities, and host conversations to be tracked according to their level of output (notes, comments) and interaction.

Moreover, the calculation of influence depends on the subjects addressed in these places of influence and the level of criticality that follows from them. Is a subject that is risky for the brand processed in accordance with specific tonality? Is the production of discourses and discussions as a whole generally favorable or critical toward the brand? It is from the meeting of these two dimensions – the importance of sources and the criticality of the topics addressed – that the web's opinion ecosystem results.

To define the importance of the sources of a web opinion ecosystem, two key indicators can be used:

- *Relevance:* This subjective qualitative indicator is based on an in-depth study of the source and its ability to produce content that makes sense of the themes of the subject. It takes into account the identity of the source, its legitimacy, and its credibility on the web in the world of monitoring. Thus, in defining this variable, notions such as qualified awareness of the source in the domain, the function and status of its author(s), and the capacity to produce content of value (exclusivity/quality) are taken into account. Each of a project's sources can be assigned a relevance rating.
- *Resonance:* This objective quantitative indicator takes into account the source's intensity of activity and its potential to retrieve the information disseminated. On the web, as with any social network, influence is primarily based on mutual recognition. It is this logic that allows a blogger or a member of Twitter to be visible to a greater or lesser extent in search engines, for example. In defining this variable, we take into account notions such as its relative audience, the frequency and volume of its publications, its capacity to generate comments and volumetry, its web ranking scores (Page Rank Google, Yahoo links, the number of RSS

flow readers), and the number of fans or followers it has. Here again, for each of a project's sources, a resonance rating can given.

From these two indicators, relevance and resonance, a total importance score for each source can be deduced, using the following formula:

Importance = relevance × resonance

The second point to work on is the identification and rating of the criticality of the opinion themes monitored. To define the criticality of the subject monitored, two key indicators can be used:

- *Risk:* This subjective qualitative indicator is based on the a priori assessment of the potential level of risk for the brand of the subject being monitored. The definition of this indicator is based on sharing knowledge as regards the brand topics to be monitored. Hence, for each subject of a project, one can assign a risk score.
- *Tonality:* This objective qualitative indicator reflects, for each note or comment processed, an overall synthesis between the leanings of the opinions expressed and the connotation register of the speaker (support, criticism, doubt, questioning). Thus, when describing each note or comment processed, we assign a tonality score on a scale from positive to negative.

From these two indicators, risk and tonality, a total criticality score for each opinion can be deduced, using the following formula:

Criticality = risk × tonality

Ultimately, it is by means of a calculation based on multiplying the importance of the source and the criticality of the opinion that we can define, opinion by opinion (and therefore subject by theme and subtheme monitored), an overall influence score.

Influence score = importance (relevance × resonance)
× criticality (risk × tonality)

To conclude, we can note the emergence today of universal social influence scoring systems, of which Klout score (www.klout.com) is the most significant (ahead of those of PeerIndex, Kred and Empire Avenue). Rather than engage in a lengthy criticism of Klout Score, nonetheless we can note some of its limitations:

- Lack of transparency in the calculation rules; thus, at the end of October 2011, all its users saw their score drop by 10–20 points, with no explanation.
- Too greater a predominance of activity in the social media, without taking into account the relevance of what is said. For example, Klout described me as an influence on the United Nations the day I wrote these lines, which is a total mystery.
- Upgrading of all social activities without real consideration of the particularity of each platform.
- Failure to take into account qualitative aspects, such as the transmission of context or offline credibility.

It should also be emphasized that, whether for our calculation system or Klout, taking account of the influence of an individual and/or a brand, without measuring its perception by its public, remains an incomplete exercise.

Key metrics

Relevance of sources, resonance of sources, tonality of opinions, and criticality of subjects.

Action objectives: anchoring the measurement of earned media in the "physical" life of the brand

Action objectives, if they can be measured correctly, allow one to construct ROI models of earned media, by bringing together all the efforts made in terms of the physical reality of selling, conversion, and subscription. However, given the lack of social commerce best practices and thinking about this relatively new subject, envisaging an effectiveness measure of earned media and their real impact (and not their assumed impact, as in analytic studies of the influence of contact points conducted to date)[9] in terms of action can only be done by questioning people in earned media ecosystems and gathering their opinions and especially their intentions regarding changes in purchasing behavior, following or in conjunction with exposure, sharing, or comments on earned media efforts implemented by the brand.

Since early 2011, experts in the field have been struggling to define complex calculation systems, leading to measures of fan value, ranging from a few dollars to over 100 dollars, and in making questionable assumptions regarding the origin of these different methods of calculation, all of them seem to omit a few simple rules, which it is important to remember.

Five main rules should be taken into account when considering the ROI of social media, and Facebook in particular.

1 Each brand has different fans: the calculated value of the fans of one brand is not necessarily applicable to the fans of another brand.
2 Each fan has a unique value: within the same page, one is addressing different individuals. Everyone is unique in their relationship to the brand.
3 Value is not the same thing as the cost of acquisition: this is a narrow view that limits value strictly to the cost of acquisition.
4 Value depends on the fan's purchasing capacity: today or tomorrow a fan may become a customer or a referring customer/prospect, which directly effects their current and potential value.
5 Value is therefore elastic over time: unless one considers that the link and relationship forged with a fan does not change over time.

These observations make it clear that it is important to consider the manner and value of collecting data, which will make good missing information with regard to knowledge about fans.

For this reason, since 2010, companies such as CRM Metrix and Millward Brown have developed tools for collecting opinions from the users of Facebook, Twitter, forums and blogs, in order to provide metrics appropriate to such objectives. Over the past three years, more than 150 pages of Facebook fans have been studied by CRM Metrix, using a standardized approach that can define benchmarked scores. This approach is based on understanding, through a system combining questioning and observations of Facebook Insights analytics data.

Three behavior dimensions provide insight into the profiles and expectations of fans with regard to the brand and its page:

- *Fan profiles:* as well as further sociodemographic data, understanding the relationship to the brand and the category, and the influence profile.
- *Fan motivations:* as well as an understanding of likes and comments, identification of engagement levers.
- *User experience:* as well as measuring participation in the various animations on the page, assessment of the different forms of relation offered by the brand.

Three effectiveness dimensions shed light on the impact of the presence of the brand on Facebook, among its fans:

- *Customer relationship management (CRM) impact:* Does the brand succeed in targeting and creating loyalty in customers and prospects?
- *Branding impact:* Does the brand succeed in developing certain brand equity dimensions?
- *Business impact:* Is the brand able to use its page as a point of entry into a digital conversion funnel (signing up for a newsletter or any other CRM program, leaving an email address, or directly purchasing online)?

The key lessons to remember from the CRM Metrix experience with regard to action objectives are:

- *A quarter of fans discovered the page through the brand website:* a logic of traffic management and leads can therefore operate between these two areas, if the brand is able to correctly redirect its fans, so as to acquire more of them.

- *Fan pages only attract true fans of the brand:* 35–60 percent of fans are promoters of brands (high recommendation level). Levels of engagement upstream of likes are therefore variable and involve positioning and suitable brand discourses.
- *User-generated content created by other fans has greater viral potential:* social recommendations have most effect in exchanges between fans, a lever that must be activated and used relevantly.
- People who share the most in a community are those who have a *better opinion of the brand:* identifying and working with such ambassadors in particular is crucial for strengthening the brand's engagement level.

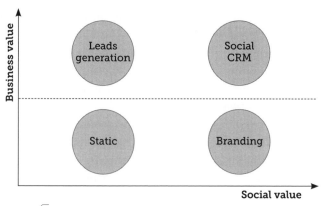

FIGURE 6.5 / Typology of Facebook pages

Source: CRM Metrix.

These findings allowed a typology to be drawn up of fan pages and the action objectives to be measured. This typology, shown in Figure 6.5, is built around two main axes:

- *Social value:* this results from the measurement of fans' inclination to interact with the brand (level of involvement), their relationship to the brand (engagement and proximity with the brand), and their brand and page recommendation level (socialization vectors).

- *Business value:* this results from the measurement of existing and potential conversion/consumption levels for the brand, as well as from knowledge of consumption modes and conversion locations (traffic destination, since conversion does not necessarily occur in Facebook).

There are various operational implications of this typology in terms of ROI:

- A page with no real social and business value with regard to its fans should review its presence strategy and reorient its traffic in the short term to another point of contact.
- A page with high social value but low business value, for example luxury brands, should orient its strategy toward a logic of working on branding and strong items, allowing it to maintain its brand equity.
- Conversely, a brand with high business value but low social value (a question of engagement by theme in multi-page strategies: it manages to attract customers but not necessarily to make them adhere to the theme) has potentially created a reservoir of leads that it will work on to convert on Facebook or elsewhere.
- A page that has managed to build up the twofold position of quality of business targeting and strong social engagement is in an interesting position for thinking about its Facebook strategy, within a more global CRM social logic, enabling it to recruit, commit, and create loyalty among prospects and valued customers.

These fan page strategies are not sealed off from each other, and can evolve over time and with regard to the orientations of brand presence on Facebook (increased number of pages, new investments). However, this typology is now effective for brands that wish to deepen their knowledge of their fans within a real perspective of measuring their ROI and their action objectives.

In addition, this measurement system is also effective for other earned media contact points and activities. Knowledge of the value of interacting with individuals combined with the value of their social involvement is crucial for evaluating business effectiveness.

> **Key metrics**
>
> Existing purchase and future purchase intention of the brand, net promoter score, attachment to and liking the brand, involvement motivations in earned media, and potential conversion locations.

Having reviewed all the metrics and KPIs specific to each of the major types of media, in Chapter 7 we show that digital marketing must be part of a global, that is, integrated, brand communication and marketing approach. In it, we describe the different stages of the implementation of an integrated marketing communication (IMC) process.

Key points

1. Presence objectives of a brand in the earned media must be determined by the uses that consumers make of the various social media platforms, forums, and blogs, including social networks such as Facebook and Twitter and video and photo-sharing platforms. In all cases, the brand will seek to initiate and engage consumers in conversations and/or measure the content of existing conversations.

2. As for the other points of contact (paid and owned), the measurement metrics and KPIs can be organized around each AIDA stage. Often "proxies" more than metrics, updated KPIs enable one to understand, approximate, and ultimately progress in the management of brand presence in the earned media.

3. Quantitative indicators (number of fans and followers, number of mentions, and so on) and qualitative indicators (tone, tonality, sentiment, content, and so on) are complementary and allow the effects to be understood.

Particular care is needed to correctly define and limit the scope of observation. Without this precaution, the measurement process can be laborious, poorly understood, and ultimately of little use.

Notes

1 Forrester (2011) *Forrester Research Interactive Marketing Forecast by Industry, 2011 to 2016 (US)*, September 2.

2 Semiocast (2012) Twitter reaches half a billion accounts: more than 140 millions in the U.S., July 30, http://semiocast.com/publications/2012_07_30_Twitter_reaches_half_a_billion_accounts_140m_in_the_US?lg=fr.

3 YouTube Statistics, www.youtube.com/yt/press/statistics.html.

4 Hewlett-Packard Case Study, Creating 2,000+ brand advocates in two weeks with LinkedIn Recommendation Ads, http://marketing.linkedin.com/sites/default/files/pdfs/LinkedIn_HPCaseStudy2011.pdf.

5 *Forrester European Technographics Online Benchmark Survey, Q3 2011.*

6 Blanchard, O. (2011) *Social Media ROI: Managing and Measuring Social Media Efforts in Your Organization*, QUE. His blog can be found at http://thebrandbuilder.wordpress.com/.

7 DDB-OpinionWay (2011) Study of the fans of brands on Facebook, www.opinion-way.com/pdf/110916_ddb-opinionway_fans_de_marques_sur_facebook_version_courte.pdf.

8 PageLever (2011) Most Facebook pages reach only 3%–7.5% of their fans, July 14, http://pagelever.com/fan-pages-impressions-pageviews-benchmark-methodology/.

9 See, for example, the MCA studies or Market ContactAudit® from Integration Marketing Communication Inc., www.integration-imc.com.

part 3

Digital marketing in the service of brand and business development

Highly specific, but far from isolated, digital marketing fits into the overall strategy of a brand. In the same way as marketing in other media, it aims to develop the business and its place in integrated marketing communication (IMC), the efficient management of which is assured by setting up a "digital dashboard."

7

From 360°
communication to
integrated marketing
communication

Executive summary

- Brand communication is becoming more and more difficult, with the fragmentation of media, shrinking advertising budgets, and increasingly "ad zapping," "mediavore" consumers (those with a voracious appetite for any form of media).

- Brands can no longer communicate through 360° communication, as they no longer have the resources, and customers themselves choose their own forms of exposure to messages. As a result, communication and marketing must be integrated and organized around the customer's preferred points of contact. This is the role of integrated marketing communication (IMC), which focuses on customer needs and aims for maximum ROI, by favoring certain media over others.

Ever more difficult brand communication

Advertisers today face a real challenge. On the one hand, traditional sociodemographic characteristics have become less relevant for understanding the behavior of their various publics and segmenting markets. On the other hand, the Internet and digital media in general (all of which is, of course, one of the reasons for writing this book) create new opportunities for contact between audiences and brands, and for combinations of advertising messages and communication media.

Increasingly customer-oriented marketing

Whereas marketing in the 1970s was characterized by "product marketing," where it was a matter of selling rather than persuading consumers to purchase, today, more than ever, marketing has to be customer focused if it is to attract. Today's more informed customers choose how they would like to be approached. For brands, it is becoming extremely difficult to stand out. On average, consumers are appealed to (consciously or unconsciously) by more than 300 messages a day. So, it becomes difficult to attract the attention of customers who are increasingly selective, only paying attention to certain messages, favoring some contact points rather than others, all of which can vary depending on the situation.

Within this perspective, while 360° marketing has long advocated developing communication distributed across a maximum of media and contact points, so as to somehow "encircle" the consumer, integrated marketing communication (IMC) gives priority to the customer and their choices, and therefore opts for some contact points at the expense of others. More precisely, IMC seeks a better return on communication costs by implementing a strategy based on a channel architecture, operating in synergy and conveying consistent messages. It is determined by statistical data on customers, and their perceptions and behavior. It offers a brand the capacity to use all tools and areas of communication, boosted by digital, with a requirement for return on investment (ROI). Since IMC is focused on the consumer, its goal is to bring increased efficiency. Whereas the aim of 360° communication is the utilization and synergy of all points of contact between the consumer and the brand, IMC seeks to go further by analyzing the relevance of and return on every touchpoint, based on an in-depth analysis of consumer behavior.

Increasingly "mediavore" consumers

How we access and consume information has undergone rapid change over the past few years. The rise of platforms, including Google, YouTube, Netflix, Facebook, Twitter, and the BBC iPlayer, as well as the introduction of new devices, such as netbooks, IPTV (Internet protocol TV), smartphones, tablets and connected/smart TVs, have fundamentally affected how many of us now use and interact with media. Given that all of these appeared in the past decade, as we look forward to 2020, many expect even greater change as the acceleration of new technologies increases.

While some of the new platforms and devices that will have an impact are yet to be invented, many others are already in development and being planned for mainstream roll-out. As such, there are several impending shifts already visible as we look at the future of media consumption. Many consumers are becoming "device agnostic" – moving from one media to another, and enlarging contact points to access content and information – causing global media habits to evolve rapidly. Device agnostic consumers have dramatically increased their content consumption by switching from one channel to another. A recent study in the USA,[1] for example, found that:

> consumers in their 20s ("digital natives") switch media venues about 27 times per nonworking hour – the equivalent of more than 13 times during a standard half-hour TV show … All participants in the study wore biometric belts that monitored their physical responses as they used media throughout more than 300 hours' worth of nonworking time. They also wore glasses with embedded cameras that kept track of what platform they used and for how long. Though hardly definitive, the research paints a worrisome picture for marketers in a world where consumers turn from screen to screen in search of something that captures and retains their attention, yet often cannot find it.

On this topic, Médiamétrie's 2011 *Media in Life* study has traced the evolution of French people's media behavior and consumption since 2005. Year after year, the French increase their contacts with the media.

In 2010, people living in France had, on average, no less than 41 contacts with digital media and entertainment every day, an increase of 7 percent compared to 2008. All age groups are affected, although it is among 18–24-year-olds that this phenomenon is most pronounced, related to their increased use of the Internet and smartphones. Clearly, today's youth are "mediavores." They enjoy a diversity of media: in the course of a single day, nearly a third of French people are in contact with at least five major media (TV, radio, print, Internet, and cinema). In 2008, the figure was a quarter.

The "classic" media – television, radio, press, and cinema – dominate the media landscape, since almost all the population (99 percent) are in contact with at least one of them in a day. The various forms of digital entertainment – video, landline, and mobile phone, music and video games – also have a huge following, with three out of every four French people accessing them every 24-hour period. Digital entertainment is engaged in regularly throughout the day, unlike mainstream media, which are characterized by high prime-time consumption.

Not specific to the so-called "developed countries," this situation can be extended, and is in fact further true for the developing economies and, specifically, Brazil, Russia, India, and China, where above average adoption of mobile devices and social networks accelerates the trend of "mediavore" consumers.

A large number of contact points with specific and complementary roles

The multiplicity of media contacts and the volatility of consumers make the principle of 360° communication increasingly less appropriate. First, the consumer prefers certain media rather than others, and second, the dramatic rise of media budgets means that advertisers have to make choices, since their budgets are less elastic. So they have to focus on the most effective points of contact. The Internet has not only changed the media landscape, but has had a huge impact on interpersonal communication – initially through forums and blogs, and more recently through social networks such as Facebook, but also Twitter, and LinkedIn for more professional relationships. Hence, although it has always been effective, word of mouth is Internet users' increasingly preferred way of relaying information. Brands are therefore obliged to "participate in these conversations," as participation more than communication is gradually becoming necessary as the new marketing procedure. A recent survey of four thousand consumers, conducted in Canada and the USA, confirms this trend (Table 7.1). Consumers were asked to rank a list of touchpoints within a selection of categories, and Table 7.1 highlights the top six most common touchpoints. For consumers, word of mouth (friends and family) is the most influential touchpoint on all the product categories considered, ranging from luxury cars through to food and cleaning products. Another interesting finding, among digital touchpoints, is that the brand's website proves to be a key touchpoint, and the most important for influencing consumers' purchases and their search for information. While the brand needs to participate in conversations on the Internet, cultivating and expanding its presence on social networks, the brand website remains a priority focal point for maintaining and developing the relationship to the brand and the company and especially for making available information sought by Internet users.

A remarkable additional finding in this study, on the four impact dimensions studied – influence, information, relationship, and trust – is that social network contact points never appear among the leading group of preferred touchpoints. Word of mouth, experts, and the brand website are the most favored touchpoints. However, some experts in the field argue that although Facebook and Twitter do not explicitly appear in this leading group, they do in fact feed word of mouth and are therefore crucial, in terms of impact, for trust and influence. It is also true that the study is dated 2011, but the same study repeated during the second semester of 2012 confirms that social networks gained ground, but not yet to the level of other traditional touchpoints identified in 2011.

TABLE 7.1 Ranking of touchpoints identified as purchase influencers*

Total Canada		Quebec Only		Rest of Canada		USA	
Friend/Family	60%	Friend/Family	55%	Friend/Family	61%	Friend/Family	59%
Professional/Specialist	43%	Professional/Specialist	43%	Display/Demo	44%	TV	38%
Display/Demo	43%	Display/Demo	40%	Professional/Specialist	43%	Display/Demo	37%
Flyer/Brochure	38%	Flyer/Brochure	38%	Flyer/Brochure	38%	Professional/Specialist	37%
TV	30%	TV	32%	TV	29%	Flyer/Brochure	25%
Website	20%	Newspaper	21%	Website	21%	Website	24%
Newspaper	19%	Website	19%	Newspaper	18%	Newspaper	18%
Magazine	14%	Magazine	15%	Magazine	13%	Magazine	12%
Radio	6%	Online ad	7%	Radio	6%	Online ad	11%
Infomercial	5%	Infomercial	6%	Email	5%	Email	8%
Online ad	5%	Radio	6%	Infomercial	4%	Radio	7%
Email	4%	Outdoor	5%	Online ad	4%	Infomercial	6%
Blogs	3%	Email	4%	Blogs	3%	Online video	4%
Outdoor	3%	Blogs	3%	Celebrity	3%	Blogs	4%
Online video	3%	Online video	3%	Online video	2%	Outdoor	3%
Celebrity	3%	Celebrity	2%	Outdoor	2%	Facebook	3%
Facebook	2%	Facebook	1%	Facebook	2%	Celebrity	2%
Twitter	1%	Twitter	1%	Twitter	1%	Twitter	2%

Note: *Touchpoints that are considered within the top three most influential when making a purchase decision.
Source: Crop.[2]

Toward the emergence of IMC

The results of the above survey on the impact of different touchpoints are revealing, confirming that although digital fundamentally changes consumer behavior, the salvation of brands lies in the complementarity of the impact and effect of different media and, more generally, different touchpoints. Even inherently Internet brands, such as Google and Amazon, cannot dispense with "touching" their prospects and customers across all available contact points. The aim is not so much to put all these contacts end to end and carry out campaigns in one medium after another, but rather to organize communication by focusing on the consumer. Whereas 360° communication emphasized consistent messages across all available media (mainstream and nonmainstream), IMC is a new, more ambitious approach, which starts from more "scientific"[3] knowledge of the consumer and goes much further in terms of selecting channels, budgetary allocations, and creativity. As such, digital marketing, like the other points of contact, is only one solution, an option to be put at the service of the brand and to fit into an overall marketing communications plan.

Although conceptually straightforward, IMC results in a real revolution throughout the marketing communication value chain.

A certain incompatibility between traditional marketing organizations and IMC

The entire value chain has been called into question. The traditional specifications for the creation and dissemination of a message in a medium is replaced by the development of a message, a "big idea" as the ad agencies put it, which will be transmitted on each of the priority consumer points of contact. Simple consistency across the various media is no longer sufficient; the message must be adapted to consumer needs and at every stage of the buying process, from upstream to downstream.

It is clear that the way advertisers have tended to organize themselves in recent years is not necessarily appropriate. This organization is generally structured around different areas of marketing skills: communication, advertising, Internet, direct marketing. This is certainly a legitimate organization, with the expertise needed to implement them, but if we accept that everyone is addressing one and the same target – the customer – such an organization very quickly reaches its limits. Similarly, budgets are often split between different decision-makers. The advent and emergence of digital gradually leads to a questioning of the relevance of compartmentalized organizations. The boundaries between advertising and direct marketing, sales promotion, direct communication, partnerships, events, and PR no longer make much sense. Digital adds other touchpoints to the panoply of customer points of contact, such as email marketing, keyword and SEO management, display, social networks, and brand content.

Marketing has never been so complicated, but it has never been more exciting. One thing is sure, the silo organizational model is coming apart and giving way to a more bottom-up approach, organized around the consumer, where expertise is integrated into the creation of the most favorable "customer experience," at all stages of the persuasion or relationship process (in the AIDA sense, for example). Moreover, it is indisputable that without change, or rather without a profound reorganization of the value chain, advertisers and agencies will not be able to survive and will give way to new brands and agencies that have succeeded in organizing themselves around the customer.

From this standpoint, it is intuitively evident that pure player companies, arising from and operating through the Internet, are better equipped, because they are inherently organized "around the customer."

> The best example is perhaps Amazon. Everything is organized around the customer. Unlike mail order companies, the managed database is structured around customers and not around the products sold. The difference is substantial and calls for a massive reorganization of the activities of traditional mail order companies.

In the case of Amazon, even if the value proposition seems relatively simple from the outside, it requires discipline, design, and deployment of considerable resources to continuously serve its customers proactively. In fact, the company is now not only a leader in e-commerce, but also in general commerce and business services; all with the same goal of serving customers better, both its own and those of partner businesses (via hosting services and cloud computing, of which Amazon was the pioneer and is the leader today). In our view, we are only at the beginning of the Amazon empire.[4]

――――――――――――――――――――――――――――――――――――

"**April 30 2013:** The World Federation of Advertisers (WFA)[5] has unveiled new research detailing the specific challenges that the world's largest advertisers are having in developing integrated marketing communications (IMC).

IMC has been named as a top priority by 80% of advertisers surveyed by the WFA in April 2013. This research has taken key areas critical to the development of IMC and identified marketers' key priorities as well as their current capabilities.

The gaps between the priorities and capabilities have been used to identify the key challenges posed by IMC in three crucial pillars: people, process and performance.

The results show that the biggest gaps remain around people and performance with the top five areas for improvement identified as follows:

1 *Setting the right KPIs (performance):* Marketers need a better idea of what success looks like to help them measure the right metrics. This is a particular challenge for single brand companies and those with an annual global ad spend of less than $500m.

2 *Demonstrating ROI (performance):* Marketers need to be able to show that integrated marketing delivers financial results. The world's biggest marketers – those spending more than $2bn annually – have most work to do in this area.

3 *Leadership (people):* To ensure company-wide adoption, a top-down approach is critical. Based on our sample, this is the top challenge for the world's largest companies. In terms of sectors, those in the food and drinks industry have (on average) the furthest to go to align leadership behind an IMC approach.

4 *Resource (people):* Companies must recruit and empower dedicated, specialized and experienced teams of staff to lead IMC efforts. Our scorecard shares that the biggest gap to bridge is amongst the biggest spending companies.

5 *Generating big ideas (process):* Companies still struggle to develop processes that help them develop unifying marketing ideas that can work across multiple channels. Companies with a single brand are lagging here when compared to companies with more complex brand portfolios

The research found that companies with an average annual ad spend of between $500 million and $2bn per year are most IMC ready, followed by the largest companies, those spending more than $2bn a year. Smaller companies are most likely to struggle.

The complexity of a company's brand portfolio appears to have little impact on IMC readiness but companies in durables and semi durables tend to perform best, followed by nondurables such as FMCG and pharma products. The next place is taken by food and drink producers. **"**

The five indispensable stages for implementing IMC

Various studies and my own consulting experience suggest that advertisers and marketing providers should adopt a five-stage procedure. This process successively requires:

- accurate knowledge of the customer shared within the company
- setting figure-based (business) and enhanced company reputation objectives
- decompartmentalization of communication disciplines and establishing arbitration rules
- a single communication plan, covering the channels that have been deemed relevant
- a dashboard to track results over time, both in terms of business impact and company reputation impact.

Stage one: "think customer"

If the essence of marketing is to serve the customer, it may seem obvious that acquiring knowledge of the customer, and particularly knowledge shared within the company, is a natural approach. My day-to-day experience, stretching back more than 20 years, tends to show that even today this supposition is by no means always well founded. For example, we often ask our advertising clients: "When was the last time you talked with, visited, 'experienced' your customers?" In most cases, the answers are vague, because too often, unfortunately, marketing managers do not know enough about their customers. How, then, can one blame the company for lacking a "customer orientation?" In reality, the impetus must come from the top of the company, because the most successful companies are often those whose CEO is "obsessed" with customer satisfaction.

Amazon

Jeff Bezos, Amazon's founder and CEO, believes that if Amazon works properly, customers should have no reason to talk to it. Conversely, all comments, feedback, and voluntary inputs are carefully analyzed to understand and continuously improve the quality of service.

Zappos

Acquired by Amazon in 2009, Zappos has the same business model, but pushed to extremes. The Zappos philosophy is one of "delivering happiness" to its customers. Founded in 1999, Zappos originally sold shoes and clothing on the Internet; today, the company plans to sell whatever meets the various needs and desires of its customers, so as to make them "happy."

For both Amazon and Zappos, from the outset their businesses have been organized around their customers and not, as is generally the case, around products.

So, the idea is not so much to sell a product as to get it to be bought by a customer. The result is admittedly the same, but the organization involved in arriving there is different. Whereas in the first case, the philosophy is a product-centered mix, in the second case, the mix is guided by the contact points that are most important to the customer/consumer at each stage of the buying cycle, from searching for information through to the purchase itself and the post-purchase phase.

We have already shared some findings of different studies that detail media and nonmedia points of contact, which are most important in the information search, purchase, post-purchase, and relationship stages. From the analysis of this information, priority contact points are selected to be used and preferred for each stage of the "customer journey." Logical enough, you say, but the approach requires that certain points of contact are favored to the detriment of others that are sometimes more naturally used by the brand or its advertising agency. It is a matter of putting aside the assumptions about the operation or impact of a particular medium and allowing the customer alone to guide one's choices. It then becomes important that the process be understood and shared by everyone in the company. To further illustrate this necessity, we present the recommendations of the Union des Annonceurs (Advertisers Union):[6]

> Although this is obvious in marketing, what counts above all is the approach that consists of truly and intimately understanding the customer in his relationship with the product. Everything flows from this information: objectives, points of contact, the nature and even the tone of messages. It is therefore a matter of exploring all the company's customers and grouping them into "strategic families" consistent with its business strategy, but who will then be addressed in a differentiated manner, in accordance with each family's specificity.

This new reality has been made popular by Google and its "zero moment of truth" (ZMOT) concept,[7] which states that whereas consumers used to choose what to buy at the shelf (echoing the well-known "first moment of truth" developed by P&G in 2005), they now research online first, often making up their minds before they get to the store. This ZMOT provides a crucial shift that marketers need to account for in their planning.

Stage two: setting detailed objectives (with figures)

Even before the emergence of IMC, setting objectives was already paramount in any communication process. Indeed, without clear and shared objectives, there is little chance of controlling the effects and thus the effectiveness of actions. In the context of IMC, setting detailed objectives goes beyond simply monitoring the satisfactory operation of a campaign. Knowing that the message is understood is certainly important in relation to its effect, but if the message is not relevant, it is unlikely to have an effect on customers/consumers. Because it is based on precise knowledge of customers and their needs, IMC should set ambitious goals and targets, both in terms of business and image. The AIDA model can serve as a reference point for defining the key indicators of the success of IMC. In particular, IMC will emphasize the updating of performance indicators, whether qualitative or quantitative, in the desire and action stages. The important thing is being able to measure, so as to monitor and thus acquire the means to advance the brand and the company.

Here are some examples of possible objectives in the desire and action stages for an IMC campaign:

- improving the brand's conversion rates, consideration rates, and purchase rates, by raising them from 40 to 45 percent
- increasing purchase intention from 30 to 35 percent
- developing a new consumption opportunity
- enhancing the brand/company reputation by one percentage point.

In general, it is less the specific effect of one medium in relation to another that will be assessed and more the overall contribution of all the contact points used. Hence, it is media synergies that will be developed and the specific contribution of digital to achieving the objectives of the IMC campaign.

Stage three: decompartmentalization of communication disciplines and establishing arbitration rules

The system of communication service providers – advertising agencies, digital communication agencies, CRM providers, PR agencies – is now organized in order to design and produce specific types of service as a priority: advertising campaigns, websites, and direct marketing campaigns. With few exceptions, this is mirrored in the way advertisers are organized, which, for their part, feature advertising services, Internet, and CRM, sometimes under the same authority, but often operating independently. But Internet management is still often incorporated into information systems management.

The sole merit of this situation is that the growing complexity of communication businesses justifies the presence of specialists on both sides. With the coming of IMC, the major drawback of such an organization is the potential lack of neutrality, since each bearer of knowledge (both on the advertiser's side and on the agency's) is in a position to best "sell" its type of service, regardless of its relevance to the promotion of the product and the specific modus operandi of the advertiser.

This lack of neutrality of service providers and decision-makers with regard to communication techniques applies equally to the channel or touchpoints that need to be chosen. The advertising agency never recommends CRM, any more than the brand's advertising manager ever recommends a PR campaign. Yet IMC implies that communication techniques and channels are chosen in accordance with measurable objectives, and set according to the habits, motivations, and needs of customers, without necessarily having the means to achieve them. The company, and particularly the marketing department, should no longer be the prisoner of their organization and their silos. It is up to them, through a change in behavior, that the stakeholders, agencies, and internal teams, once the issue is clearly defined, consider the appropriateness of their technique or communication channel, in the light solely of its effectiveness and customer needs.

IMC strongly disrupts organizations. We often say that organizations do not change overnight, and that change is a process. We therefore recommend introducing things gradually, in particular testing everything on a specific operation and devising a new form of team organization.

> The formation of a project team allows all the internal experts involved in the operation to be brought together under the authority of the marketing director. To celebrate the 100th anniversary of its brand in 2008, Lesieur (which manufactures and sells edible oils and dressings) set up IMC around the project with a cross-functional organization, which required the collaboration of the entire business.

Reorganization does not, however, mean getting rid of all a company's expertise. It is recommended that expertise should be called on accord-

ing to what the project concerned requires. Everything seems possible, subject to three conditions:

- *The creation of a new state of mind:* this requires expert structures (advertising, direct marketing, the Internet) to justify, in each case, the relevance of their intervention, depending on the customer, goals, and ROI.
- *The creation of a strong arbitration procedure:* in principle, it is the role of the chief marketing officer (CMO) to mediate between the expert structures. For them, this is the way to regain a strong position in the company, based on the success of their actions and traditional marketing's two areas of expertise – knowledge of the customer and communication skills. The CMO may also rely on a specialized board-type organization, which will recommend a channel architecture or points of contact.
- *A change in budgetary rules:* it seems obvious that setting and allocating budgets by discipline or expertise is devastating for the creation of value, starting with that of the customer. Moreover, some departments often feel "obliged" to spend, on the pretext that if they do not, they will not be allocated the same budget next year. Conversely, it is essential to have a centralized budget, which will be released to the expert entities concerned, based on justified expenditure for each operation.

EXPERT VIEWPOINT

Oscar Jamhouri
CEO of Integration Marketing and Communications

Marek Winiarz
MD of MeTHOD™

Integration is the only global company that has been measuring integrated marketing communication for over 15 years. What measurement purpose does your MCA®[8] proprietary research primarily serve?

All current techniques measure what the consumer receives. Traditional media surveys give marketers insights into the potential reach, frequency, and gross ratings points of their advertising plans and those of their competitors. Recently, marketers have also been increasingly turning to stochastic research in an attempt to assess the communication weight of competitive marketing activities, beyond mass media.

The inherent weakness of this approach to contact measurement lies in the fact that it measures weight and efficiency of dollars spent in a given category, rather than the effectiveness of marketing activity. Furthermore, it is almost impossible on a regular basis to keep track of all brand activities that go into a market.

Against this specific background, Integration developed the Market ContactAudit®. One of the principal benefits of MCA® is that it avoids the complications and inherent weaknesses of conventional systems, and does so by observing consumers' consumption of contacts (or touchpoints) in a given category and market, and further, their associations of brands with such contacts.

By knowing which type of contact the consumer most values, brand managers can tailor their messaging efforts to the contact points they know to be the most influential in building consumer brand engagement. By definition, this provides the most effective and efficient brand experience strategy.

Although metrics and KPIs may greatly vary per media, contact or touchpoint, what are the key concepts you want brands to pay attention to?

MCA metrics per media, contacts or touchpoints do vary by markets, categories, and target groups. Using a common currency system, MCA metrics are linked to deliver a validated chain of the following indicators:

- the influence of each/all contacts, reported in a common currency

- the capacity to differentiate each and every contact
- the brand ability to engage through each and every contact
- the brand ability to mix contacts in order to deliver the most engaging brand experience.

Integration studied each of its MCA indicators to validate the entire data chain, and from the same metrics delivered:

- The KPI for the management of the enterprise
- The diagnostics indicators for the brand and marketing communication experts.

The KPIs for the management of the enterprise report on the fundamental contribution of marketing to the business and they are unambiguously connected to the dollars:

1 How well are we engaging our customers?
2 How well are we converting engagement into sales?
3 How cost efficient is the marketing function?

The diagnostics indicators for the brand and marketing communication experts are a level down from executive dashboards and contain information on causes (factors) that determine the outcome of brand engagement. Full treatment of these indicators is beyond the scope of this interview and can be found in detail in the *MCA Handbook* (www.integration-imc.com).

To your knowledge, is there one magic bullet KPI that could measure the impact and ROI of marketing?

Marketing ROI is an elusive measure that the marketing community has been struggling with for a long time, and the fact that we don't have an accepted method is not for lack of trying. Much has been attempted, various models have been proposed by respected consultants and yet, after all this effort, we are still searching. Let me go out on the limb here and postulate that traditional ROI measures – ratio of profit to equity – are not possible for marketing. I offer no proof other than the observation that if a formula existed, it would have been found by now – after all the effort and expense devoted to it by brilliant minds in the past few decades.

The reason is that while marketing expense can be captured, marketing outcome cannot be tied to profitability in any "hard-wired" way. Profits are a result of many factors that include "money in" and "money out". In six sigma terminology, profit is an outcome designated as Y, which depends on many factors, called x. In mathematical shorthand: $Y = f(x_1, x_2, \ldots x_n)$. Marketing is only one factor (x) among many and not a very prominent one. Marketing contribution is confounded by other, faster acting, more direct factors. Marketing is just one of the factors in sales and it's a long road from "sales" to "profits."

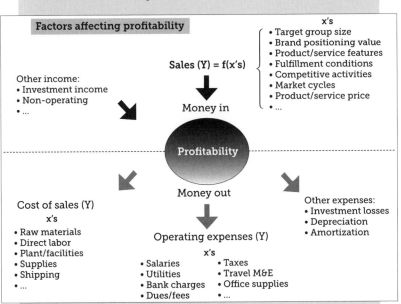

Factors affecting profitability

x's
- Target group size
- Brand positioning value
- Product/service features
- Fulfillment conditions
- Competitive activities
- Market cycles
- Product/service price
- ...

Sales (Y) = f(x's)

Money in

Other income:
- Investment income
- Non-operating
- ...

Profitability

Money out

Cost of sales (Y)
x's
- Raw materials
- Direct labor
- Plant/facilities
- Supplies
- Shipping
- ...

Operating expenses (Y)
x's
- Salaries
- Utilities
- Bank charges
- Dues/fees
- Taxes
- Travel M&E
- Office supplies
- ...

Other expenses:
- Investment losses
- Depreciation
- Amortization

FIGURE 7.1 Factors affecting profitability

Factors affecting profitability

Contribution to profitability by marketing activities is, at most, a second order effect, unlike manufacturing where costs have an immediate, direct effect. For example, a poor management decision in a manufacturing plant will immediately wipe out and mask any profit contribution from marketing activities. Conversely, an excellent marketing campaign effect will not show up until much later and only if other factors remain steady. Realistically, the myriad other factors are unlikely to remain steady, thus frustrating the efforts.

Nevertheless, an overwhelming majority of CMOs believe that such a measure is needed to provide marketing accountability. Since a direct connection to profitability is tenuous, "hard" numbers can be obtained by proxy.

MCA provides a proxy – real outcome not in dollars but in brand experience. Brand experience is one attribute that marketing owns – it is not shared with other functions or departments. We can call a proxy ROI a return in brand experience or yield in brand experience: a ratio of brand experience share to dollars. While this does not quantify the contribution to profitability, it can be considered a "hard" measure of marketing efficiency. If brand experience increased and costs did not, then marketing programs become more efficient. This indicator is measured in percentage change, and it is an accountable efficiency metric.

Stage four: a communication plan covering all communication channels

Given our comments so far, it is unsurprising that the communication plan has to be conceived as a whole, that is, encompassing all communication channels and contact points, each of which is placed in the service of the ICM objectives. The succession of communication plans medium by medium should be ended; the overall communication plan must be conceived and put into practice as a genuine business plan in the service of the brand. Instead of a succession of presentations from each provider, there will be a single presentation of the ICM plan, which will allow all the IMC value chain providers, especially the advertiser, to have a unified version of its communication plan.

Why? Quite simply, because it delivers an immediate and complete view of the coherence desired. "Customers are waiting for this or that need, they are thinking about it, we will convince them of whatever it may be by means of a communication campaign conveyed by such and such a point of contact." Reading and understanding the plan becomes simpler, it is easier to judge its relevance, and share it widely within the company for easier appropriation by all the departments concerned, from front office to back office by way of management. In the end, although any change in the organization of working practices is generally difficult, all the advertiser's providers and internal participants benefit from the change. The greater the fluidity of the implementation of the plan, thanks to the use of means that are truly integrated and oriented toward the attainment of common goals, the better the return on, and the value of, the contribution of each service provider (shared briefings, shared meetings, shared presentations, shared recommendations, shared responsibility), and ultimately the greater the effectiveness in terms of results.

Stage five: setting up a dashboard to track the effectiveness of results over time

Even more than traditional communications, IMC is allied to a desire for results that are more demarcated, more measurable, and ultimately more effective. Rather than simply tracking how the message is received and understood, or approved of (in the attention and interest stages of the AIDA model), IMC emphasizes tracking the impact, over time, of its effects. The dashboard is not only a monitoring tool, but also a tool for managing overall performance, by category of customer/prospect and by type of channel/point of contact. The objective is to move toward maximum ROI – and even more so in the case of the Internet, which allows day-to-day tracking of actions, and thus offers the possibility of modifying or optimizing the efficiency and effectiveness of the plan deployed.

Setting up a dashboard generally allows two levels of analysis to coexist. The first concerns the measurement of performance in general, as well as for each of the stages of the purchase decision process (in the AIDA sense, for example, from awareness to consideration, and from purchase to loyalty, by way of the image). To track progress over time, measurement should be recurrent or continuous, and closely linked to ROI. With regard to brand reputation and its evolution, the carmaker Renault estimated its reputation deficit to be €300 per vehicle compared to its main competitor, which needed to be offset by promotions. With, let's say, two million vehicles sold every year, the annual deficit could cost the company €600 million. Given this impact, quarterly or even monthly assessments should be implemented in order to effectively manage the impact of ICM on the brand image, which, in this example, represents the second level of analysis.

As well as measuring the effectiveness or ROI of a communication campaign, it is also important to assess the performance or profitability by media type or point of contact, in order to optimize the efficiency of resources used to serve the campaign objectives. Here, particularly when assessing paid or owned media, "response curve models" are a first line of research. This is a matter of comparing the evolution of sales according to the impact of endogenous variables, such as the promotion level or price, while trying to control exogenous variables that may have an impact on sales.

A second line of research concerns the linkage between the impact and the specific effect of each contact point. In this context, it is especially appropriate, for example, to use the MCA method, the results of which can provide a comprehensive diagnosis of the impact of each contact point, by market and for each of the brands in the market. The analytical approach proposed by the MCA method is to enhance the value of the brand experience point (BEP) of each of the contact points, BEP being correlated with the brand's market share.[9] Recent research from Integration[10] shows that the profile of brand experience shifts away from mass media and direct/personal contacts to the benefit of digital: from 2006 to 2012, the share of digital brand experience delivered has more than doubled, but it is useful to be reminded that point of purchase activities remain the largest source of influence for consumers, even today. To this end, it is worth noting that the capacity of digital contacts to influence consumers has not grown significantly over the years, and is still slightly below "mass media", although both are surpassed by direct/personal contacts, indirect, and point of purchase. This is shown in Figure 7.2. To quantify the influence of a contact on a brand choice, Integration use what it calls the "contact clout factor" (CCF), a composite measure of influence that includes attractiveness, information, and persuasive value.

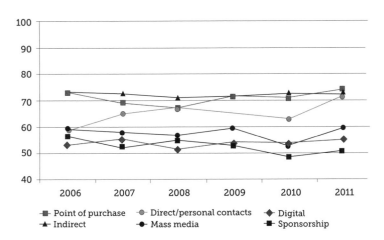

FIGURE 7.2 ╱ **CCF index by contact category**

Source: Intergration.[10]

There are many examples of results of this kind achieved by the MCA method. Integration has since specialized in the implementation of ROMI (return on marketing investment) programs, for customers using dashboard tools, which help manage the effectiveness of the marketing function as a whole. To our knowledge, the MCA method remains one of the most effective approaches for managing and controlling the impact of IMC actions, with an ability to be rolled out globally.

We will return more comprehensively to the significance, philosophy, and construction of dashboards in Chapter 8. In the meantime, remember that IMC first and foremost promotes an integrated organization, aiming at maximum effectiveness whatever the contact point or points considered. Digital media, like other media, are at the disposal of the strategy.

Key points

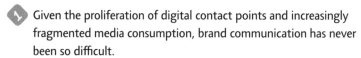 Given the proliferation of digital contact points and increasingly fragmented media consumption, brand communication has never been so difficult.

After 360° communication, which simply aims to maximize the number of contact points involved in the media plan, the future lies with integrated marketing communication (IMC), which is centered on the consumer and focuses on the best contacts rather than all of them indiscriminately.

The emergence of IMC requires the decompartmentalization of marketing and communication practices and disciplines in the company.

The implementation of IMC entails five key stages:
- think customer: to build the communication plan around selected contact points upstream and downstream of purchase
- set detailed objectives to justify the investment and to measure effectiveness
- decompartmentalize communication disciplines and establish arbitration rules to effectively prioritize certain media/contacts rather than others
- include and prioritize all communication channels
- set up a dashboard to monitor effectiveness over time.

Notes

1 Advertising Age (2012) Young consumers switch media 27 times an hour, April, http://adage.com/article/news/study-young-consumers-switch-media-27-times-hour/234008/.

2 *The Crop Touchpoints Study – Mastering the Communication Mix*, www.crop.ca/sondages/pdf/2010/Touchpoint_article01.pdf.

3 Thanks to the services of companies such as Integration Marketing and Communications Ltd and its well-known Market ContactAudit® (MCA®) technology.

4 See, for example, the excellent article in *Wired Magazine*, "Jeff Bezos owns the web in more ways than you think," www.wired.com/magazine/2011/11/ff_bezos/all/1.

5 WFA press release, WFA highlights barriers to effective integrated marketing communications,http://www.wfanet.org/en/press/press-releases/wfa-highlights-barriers-to-effective-integrated-marketing-communications?p=1.

6 Union des Annonceurs (Advertisers Union) 2011 Guide, *How Advertisers Must Put in Place Integrated Marketing Communications*, www.uda.fr.

7 For more information, visit www.zeromomentoftruth.com.

8 MCA® stands for Market ContactAudit®, Integration's proprietary research tool. Since 1997, MCA metrics have been the only validated multi-contact measurement worldwide. They correlate consistently with market share at >.80, validating the importance of MCA metrics for managing marketing communications.

9 See Cook, W. (2007) *An ARF Research Review of Integration Marketing & Communications Limited's Market Contact Audit Methodology,* which provides an assessment of the validity of the MCA method. See also www.integration-imc.com.

10 Integration Marketing and Communications (2012) *The Emergence and Rise of Digital Contacts: How the Youngest Contact Group has Become an Asset for Companies Worldwide*, May, http://static.squarespace.com/static/51fd32fbe4b0f7c27ae94c5b/t/52088f7ae4b0e286858128b4/1376292730438/Emergence%20and%20Rise%20of%20Digital%20Contacts_Official%20version.pdf.

8

Digital dashboards
A tool for managing the effectiveness of digital marketing and integrated marketing communication (IMC)

Executive summary

- The relative measurability and immediacy of digital media can give advertisers the impression that it is comparatively simple to monitor their effectiveness.
- Setting up a dashboard is a key stage for sustainably incorporating digital marketing into IMC.
- This dashboard must go beyond simply reporting and providing information that can meet detailed effectiveness monitoring objectives. A number of steps are crucial for its success, including adapting KPIs to objectives, selecting the "right" platform, and developing an optimal user interface for the full appropriation of the dashboard.

The digital dashboard: a tool in the aid of objective decision-making

The interactivity and immediacy of digital media have given users the impression of relatively easy access to information and, with regard to monitoring its effectiveness, instant access to campaign results. We have commented on this situation from the outset of this book, because we believe that it is often the source of the false impression that digital is by far the most measurable of media. We have put this impression into perspective, since the possession of large amounts of data, in real time, does not always provide data suitable for the objectives of monitoring effectiveness. Admittedly, some of this data can be incorporated into a dashboard, but a dashboard will ideally take data from different sources or information systems, and becomes not only a monitoring tool, but also a tool for managing overall performance, by customer/prospect category and by type of channel or touchpoint. When the dashboard goes beyond simply "reporting" or making available information, and includes prediction functionalities linking cause and effect, then it becomes a formidable weapon, and distinguishes those companies that make metrics and analytics in general a driving force for their performance.[1] In this chapter, we will explain:

- what a dashboard is, and what benefits it brings
- how to build a dashboard and what information it should include
- how best to use a dashboard and put it at the service of an organization.

If marketing is to win acclaim, it will do so by its ability to demonstrate its usefulness. Although marketing and communication departments complain about the relative lack of measurability of their functions, my experience as a consultant and teacher confirms that marketing people in general are not necessarily always comfortable with figures or fond of data that can reveal their ROI. However, companies that implement and use a performance dashboard see, on average, an improvement in their marketing ROI of 10–35%. But without investment in time and resources, they are unlikely to benefit from this capacity. The past 20 years may be characterized by the huge increase in the amount of data available, the so-called "big data," in real time. It is certainly becoming increasingly difficult to analyze everything, but this should not be an excuse for doing nothing, quite the contrary. Never before has technology made data and information so easily available (quite literally, at one's fingertips, through keyboard and trackpad), viewable and transportable from one connection point to another. For example, a recent study by Accenture[2] shows that 35% of marketers were planning to invest more resources in the implementation of their marketing dashboard, hand in hand with their expected level of investment in digital, since the additional resources allocated also amounted to 35%.

Why have your own dashboard?

The reason for having your own dashboard is simple: the better to control the destiny of your brand. As we have already made clear, experience shows that investment in time and resources are generally worth it: between 10% and 35% positive impact on the return of marketing investments. Although effectiveness and better performance are the ultimate goals, there are a number of advantages and benefits associated with the introduction of dashboards:

- *Improved efficiency of the means deployed:* Indeed, optimizing the allocation of resources to achieve goals is the first kind of efficiency, by having the right information promptly available. Simple, you may say, but often difficult for the silo organization of marketing and communication departments. The synergies stemming from IMC require a discipline that is crystallized in the development of a performance measurement dashboard.
- *Taking decisions in a timely manner:* We live in a hyperconnected world where the best is sometimes the enemy of the good. Knowing, understanding, and simulating in a timely manner is usually synonymous with performance. The aim is not to confuse speed with haste; the "thought-out" architecture and structure of the dashboard allows you to understand and act quickly.
- *Making the right decisions:* As we have said, it is essential to move quickly, but without rushing. The aim is often not to reinvent the decision-making process but to simplify it through the prompt provision of the right information, which will facilitate the choice of scenarios and possible adjustments.

- *Carry out effective marketing that directly impacts the business and/or the company reputation:* The aim is no longer to run "remarkable campaigns."
- *Simplifying and improving communication within the company:* Dashboards contribute to the culture of sharing and common knowledge in the business at all levels of the organization, from the personnel in contact with customers and prospects through to top management. The provision of indicators or KPIs specific to each department makes this easier. For example, on entering the e-commerce department in the headquarters of the Air France-KLM group in Amsterdam, you see a continuously updated screen that shows the KPIs of klm.com website.
- *Answering the basic questions:* Every marketing and communication department asks these questions. These are some typical examples, although the list in not exhaustive since each company will have its own particular concerns:
  - What is the relative performance of each media mix?
  - What is the contribution of each digital contact point?
  - Is the ongoing campaign consistent with the objectives set?
  - How has my conversion "funnel" performed?
  - Is the traffic recorded adequate in terms of quantity and quality?
  - How should I deploy my remaining resources in the light of these results?
  - Does the media mix chosen allow me to differentiate my brand from its competitors?

Dashboards should be able to respond to these types of questions. While often of a strategic nature, the answers given can also be tactical and operational, particularly in digital marketing; for example, refocusing and changing the layout of a homepage or landing page that does not have a satisfactory conversion rate. In all cases, the dashboard is, and must be, adapted to the needs of its users, otherwise they will not use it or not use it enough. Moreover, it is often not so much the material resources allocated but more the time spent adapting a dashboard to real operational needs that accounts for the impact it may have on the effectiveness of digital marketing and, more generally, IMC. Having reviewed the benefits of dashboards, we now turn to the question of how to build a dashboard.

The four key stages in building a dashboard

Imagine for a moment that your car doesn't have a dashboard. You could, of course, start the engine and drive off, but with no information about the fuel level, temperature, speed, and so on, it would be difficult to drive very far. All too often, digital means navigating under similar conditions. Worse still, if you have a driving licence, it is assumed that you know how to drive. But how do you manage your digital marketing without a "digital licence," without knowing how it works or what you have to do, without having clearly defined objectives and control KPIs that will help you manage its effectiveness? Absurd? Possibly, but this is typically the situation brands find themselves in when they engage in campaigns and a marketing program without having set up a suitably adapted dashboard. The good news is that with a little discipline, which begins with an alignment of KPIs to the campaign objectives implemented, the tools for organizing and visualizing data are becoming more numerous and are relatively easy to use. But tools are not everything: a good worker certainly has good tools, but the job can still be done badly unless the worker prepares it properly.

Stage one: analysis of the existing situation and alignment of KPIs with objectives

The analysis of the existing situation and alignment of KPIs with objectives is unquestionably the most important step. We definitely recommend spending more time on this stage, because if it is not done optimally, the rest will not follow. Too often, we rush to make use of any indicators whatsoever without thinking about their relevance and validity,[3] on the grounds that they're "good enough" and will do the job. No! So let's start from the beginning:

- Determine the objectives of the dashboard: state what it should be used for, as well as what it should *not* be used for.
- Identify the challenges and the gaps or shortfalls faced by the business.
- Find out how to obtain, aggregate, make available, update, and distribute information.

• Choose the metrics and indicators or KPIs that can measure your objectives in terms of the AIDA model and in terms of the efficiency of the means used. Which will help you assess the efficiency and effectiveness of the means deployed, and thus the achievement of your objectives? Can they help you diagnose the source of discrepancies between objectives and accomplishments?

Organize your metrics and KPIs around, for example, each stage of the AIDA model. These follow from the objectives assigned to digital marketing in general and to each campaign or initiative at large. In Part 2 we described the metrics most commonly associated with each stage of the persuasion model. They may also be classified by brand objectives (awareness, image, preference) or business objectives (penetration: testing, adoption, repeat purchase, and loyalty; purchase frequency; market share; and so on) (see Figure 8.1).

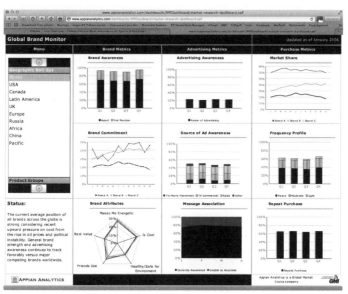

FIGURE 8.1 / **Example of dashboard with KPIs and metrics organized around various key stages of the AIDA model**

Source: Appian Analytics (Global Market Insite).

Once the most appropriate KPIs have been identified, whether quantitative, qualitative or both, you must identify the data sources that will allow you to obtain the necessary data and/or invest in the resources that will enable you to obtain the data needed to establish the KPIs deemed necessary. Having identified the data, you must then plan the structure, content, and frequency of reporting, all of which need to be adapted for each type of addressee, both internal and external. All the stakeholders should be involved at this stage. Without everyone's involvement and participation, the finest of dashboards will be stillborn, because they will be not understood, not shared, not wanted, and ultimately not used.

Stage two: refining requirements

With the KPIs aligned with the objectives, you are all set to go, but the job is not yet done. Far from it, so do not rush into constructing your dashboard without first defining the contours and needs more precisely. Each metric and KPI must be understood and developed and must be consistent with the monitoring objectives targeted. The time spent on the optimal and reasoned choice of indicators is directly correlated with success in setting up the dashboard. Without being exhaustive, we list below a number of questions that are often useful for detailing and going forward confidently in the construction of your dashboards:

- Do you have the appropriate KPIs in relation to the objectives aimed for? Do these KPIs contain both pure performance indicators and diagnostic indicators or "drivers" of performance KPIs? Often useful for understanding, explaining, and predicting, they can sometimes also prevent getting a "black box" feeling about misunderstood or unwanted KPIs. If this is the case, it is the upstream stage that is at fault, not misunderstood KPIs, and which risks the dashboard being stillborn.
- Does the dashboard user have the means to understand and assess the "level of reliability and sensitivity" of the indicators concerned? By reliability, we refer to the stability of the figures made available. Often, as we said, the available data have a "proxy" role, that is, one able to

provide early alerts about current performance trends. There is nothing more unsettling for the uninitiated than to see a KPI vary (even marginally) without the overall diagnosis changing. This is why digital ("the most measurable of media") is difficult to fully monitor: better to get closer to the truth in order to decide more calmly than to "fly by sight."

- How frequently is the available data updated and refreshed? Is this frequency well adapted to all the addressees and users of the dashboard? Is it possible to easily obtain trend histories and understand the dynamics of change over time?

- Are the KPIs of each stage of the model clearly understood and linked? In other words, is it easy to understand the role and the value of these indicators, and the links between them?

- As well as being able to monitor and assess the present situation, does the dashboard have a "forecasting" functionality? Are anticipated trends well monitored? That is, is the user sufficiently informed and knowledgeable about the potential outcome of these trends?

- Is the delivery of KPIs well "framed" by the context which ensures their legitimacy and value? In other words, is it easy to immediately understand the role and value of the KPI in relation to the objective measured in the context?

- Are the metrics, the construction of KPIs, and their meanings sufficiently explained to the user? Is it always easy to remember their content?

- What level of training is required to operate the dashboard? Are "obligatory" training sessions already in place? Is a more expert training schedule possible and available?

Stage three: choosing the "right" technological platform

You might say that choosing the "right" technological platform is simple because the essentials have already been taken care of. Not so. In fact, this is far from simple, because without an optimal choice of platform adapted to the needs of the users and their environment, the work of analysis and adaptation of the first two stages will be in vain. The choice is guided by:

- *The "data load"*: What is the volume of data exchanged? The esti-mated number of server calls? Connection requirements with internal and external sources? The level of confidentiality needed in the trans-mission of data? The locations of 24-hour access? And so on.
- *Access requirements*: How many users are there, in which geographical areas, and what levels of precision and analytical capacity are available at the user level? Are the users all internal to the company or are they also external? If there are external users, how many are there and at what security level?
- *Navigation in the dashboard itself*: Is it a single set page? What level of analysis do you go down to for each KPI? Are these levels different for different types of user (internal or external)?

Stage four: constructing the user interface

Clearly, constructing the user interface is far from straightforward. Web technologies are evolving, and users are changing and becoming increas-ingly more demanding in terms of usage requirements and ergonomics. Too often the user interfaces of dashboards are not very accessible or intuitive. Whatever the value of the content, if the information is not sufficiently "digestible," it will be little read and therefore of little use. The value of a dashboard is primarily measured by its usage value; the more intuitive the dashboard, the more it will be used. Do not hesitate if you can include an ergonomist and/or a creative in its construction. Remember with the first dashboards you build, once they are constructed, everything seems obvi-ous (the usual reactions of customers), yet there is a lot of back and forth between earlier versions and the final version. The greater the number of tracking objectives and the greater the number of tracking indicators, the more difficult the task of integrating and visualizing everything. Visualiza-tion is key, pie charts, histograms, spider graphs, and so on, are possible options, but must remain consistent from one level of the dashboard to another ("drill down menu"), while still being able to adequately repre-sent important facts and figures and, of course, in proportion to their real significance. Building a dashboard has two main difficulties: the "logical" organization of data and indicators, and their visualization. This equation is not easy to solve: the dashboard must be intuitive in terms of access and comprehension, fast loading, descriptive and predictive, "open" (able to accommodate different data sources), scalable, pleasing to look at, and so on – a true technical and creative equation. One way to represent it is to imagine a matrix with multiple entries capable of explaining everything simply while allowing one to go further in the analysis.

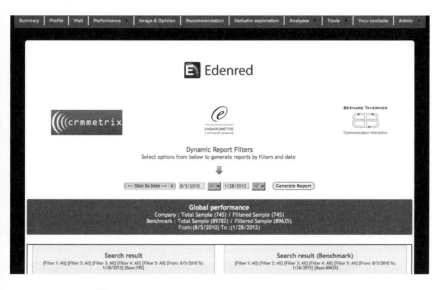

FIGURE 8.2 / The dashboard of the CRM Metrix-BTCI e-corporate barometer

A good way of representing the requirements of a well-constructed dashboard is to give some examples of functionalities available on a "good" user interface. Here, we list some of the most common functionalities, and view them through an example of a dashboard (see Figure 8.2):

• *Geography/region filters:* for visualizing results by region, country, or even city in the case of a local business.

- *"Temporal" filters:* for selecting periods specific to particular actions, for example. The reference unit is usually one day.
- *The navigation module:* providing access to the various performance modules, themselves organized, for example, around the main stages of the AIDA model.
- *Selection of KPIs:* a simple tool (click and drop) for selecting the metrics needed for monitoring the various objectives.
- *Benchmarking:* temporal (week, quarter, year) for dynamic and evolving monitoring and/or comparison with other internal and/or external data (Google Analytics industry standards, for example).
- *Sharing of insights:* for writing and sharing comments on the results with other users.
- *Visualization of data sources:* for understanding the nature and provenance of data sources.
- *Data extraction:* for exporting raw data in different formats, and the results formatted (in PDF or Excel, for example).

The aim in all cases is to make the information accessible with a single click. The more intuitive the interface, the more it will be used, and the more likely it will be to directly impact the ROI of your marketing initiatives.

As well as the functionalities listed above, a "good" dashboard also has specific sections or modules. In our opinion, two of these are crucial: "executive summary" and "analytical" modules. In some cases, other modules may also be available. For example, a "financial" module, the purpose of which is to provide information on investments by "channel" or point of contact, and monitoring of impact indicators such as sales, market share, estimate requests, and the number of incoming calls.

The "executive summary" provides a summary of the main results. Generally intended for general management or management committees, it provides an overview of the main KPIs. The executive summary is often the default homepage for accessing the dashboard. It aims to summarize all the indicators pertaining to the impact of actions in the light, for example, of the main stages of the AIDA model. It also offers, with a single click, the possibility of going into more detailed analysis of each KPI, through the modules and functionalities we described above. A survey carried out by the WFA[4] on its members in December 2011 shows that digital marketing managers of large groups believe that the ideal number of KPIs is between 5 and 10 (52% of them) or between 10 and 15 (24% of them). So, there are not necessarily very many KPIs used (between 5 and 10 on average), but they are all linked to the requirements of monitoring objectives.

The "analytical module" should, for its part, enable interested persons to go deeper into the analysis, moving from simple descriptive content to a more explanatory analysis, incorporating statistical analysis resources, such as the possibility of crossing variables, revealing correlations, drawing up trend curves, and carrying out simulations. Often relegated to second place in setting up the dashboard, it is nonetheless important to formulate early on the features and capabilities offered by the analytical module. Indeed, if the dashboard is quickly adopted by its users, some of them will soon want to have easily available tools that can help them go further in the analysis. Without this possibility, a number of frustrations may arise that will ultimately affect the successful adoption of the dashboard itself.

How P&G presents data to decision-makers[5]

"If you can establish a common visual language for data, you can radically upgrade the use of data to drive decision-making and action. The best case I can cite for this argument is Procter & Gamble, which has institutionalized data visualization as a primary tool of management. Working with visual analytics software ... P&G has put visual displays of key information on desktops — over 50,000 P&G employees now have access to a "Decision Cockpit".

In addition to the desktop displays, P&G has built meeting spaces that it calls "Business Spheres" in over 50 locations where management information is displayed for review and decision-making by groups. Some of these rooms, like the one at P&G's Cincinnati headquarters ... actually are spherical in shape, though most are conventional rectangular meeting rooms freshly outfitted with large screens on the walls.

...

Having such displays in common use is especially important to P&G because it is an extremely global company, and prefers to develop managers by moving them regularly from one brand and geographical market to another. Consistent data visualization across the corporation reflects and supports that strategy. Step into a Business Sphere in Cincinnati, Singapore, or Geneva and you'll see the same charts and graphs projected. Sit down at a desk in any P&G location, and the Decision Cockpit works the same way. P&G tries to make its graphics and colors "Apple simple" to ensure that managers can focus on the important business issues wherever they are in the world.

...

P&G's dedication to common and well-understood data displays shows what is possible when senior managers are able to stop spending so much time discussing whose data is correct, what data should really be used, and how it should best be displayed. They can spend that much more time devising ways to address the problems and opportunities. It's the creativity that is exercised on those fronts that really drives the success of businesses. ''

Recent changes triggered by the ability to obtain massive amounts of data in real time drives new opportunities and challenges to move toward what some authors call "analytics 2.0." Indeed, seismic shifts in technology and consumer behavior during the past decade have produced granular, virtually infinite records of the steps and actions consumers take online. Add to this trend the data available from digital video recorders, retail checkouts, credit card transactions, call center logs, and so on, and you can see that marketers now have access to an unimaginable amount of information about what consumers see and do. Clearly, from ROI standpoint, the opportunity is clear, but so is the challenge. Indeed, as the statistician Nate Silver puts it:[6]

> Every day, three times per second, we produce the equivalent of the amount of data that the Library of Congress has in its entire print collection. Most of it is … irrelevant noise. So unless you have good techniques for filtering and processing the information, you're going to get in trouble.

Companies such as MarketShare urge marketers to move away from analytics 1.0 measurement approaches, "which look backward a few times a year to correlates sales with a few dozen of variables" and instead use

> *analytics 2.0*, a set of capabilities that can chew through terabytes of data and hundreds of variables in real time. It allows these companies to create an ultra-high-definition picture of their market-ing performance, run scenarios, and change ad strategies on the fly … With these data-driven insights, companies can often maintain their existing budgets yet achieve improvements of 10% to 30% (sometimes more) in marketing performance.[6]

The move to analytics 2.0 involves three broad activities:

- *Attribution:* the process of quantifying the contribution of each element of advertising
- *Optimization:* or "war gaming" by using predictive analytics tools to run scenarios for business planning
- *Allocation:* the real-time distribution of resources across marketing activities according to optimization scenarios.

We agree with this move toward "analytics 2.0," but also believe that it is a matter of having the available capabilities to do so; namely, access to all possible exogenous variables to explain and detail consumer responses to IMC stimuli impact, analytical capabilities to run and maintain such processes, and, above all, the people and organizational maturity to drive and implement such a process. On this last point, as stated at the beginning of this book, we strongly believe that there are organizations that are more analytically driven than others (we used the example of P&G, that, as shown earlier in this chapter, is fully capitalizing on the new enhanced power of real-time decision-making with digital dashboards), and these organizations are more ready to move toward analytics 2.0. Other organizations still need to align culture, processes, and capabilities that will offer enhanced decision-making with data and metrics. As we have said many times, measurement is a discipline that offers high ROI when done properly. The earlier you start, the sooner you can reap the rewards. We therefore urge marketers to be inspired by analytics 2.0 rather than scared, as the future of measurement is already here.

EXPERT VIEWPOINT

Tom Davenport
Distinguished professor in information technology and management at Babson College, USA, and author of bestselling book, Competing on Analytics

Would you say that "digital" is a change agent to trigger better abilities for companies to implement analytics-driven management decisions?

Yes, it's definitely an important change agent. Companies realize that with digital marketing, all the data they need to make analytical decisions is available already, and in many cases it is relatively easy to identify the customer. They just need to capture and analyze the data. It's much harder in some other customer channels such as retail stores or call centers.

What would you say are the key barriers for analytics deployment in Fortune 1,000 companies?

> I think the greatest barrier by far is the lack of understanding of both analytics and new marketing technologies by senior executives and marketing professionals. There has been dramatic change in both areas, and there are relatively few managers – even in marketing – who are fully conversant with digital marketing, all the new platforms, testing, and the analytical tools to make better marketing decisions. We need a massive retraining effort to make this successful.

Constructing and launching the dashboard

Now that we have elaborated the various stages in building a dashboard and the most common and useful functionalities and modules, once the content is defined, it must then be assembled, constructed, and launched in the organization. The "assembly" stage often refers to the choice of technology. Choosing one platform rather than another depends on the complexity of the content. We are the first to recommend keeping things simple, since on the basis of experience, it is these that are most likely to work. It is advisable here to work with a team, agency or specialized service provider that is used to setting up dashboards. Bear in mind that the best dashboard is one that exists and is used. Once it has been assembled, the dashboard has to be launched. Plan the launch in two stages: a pilot or "beta" stage, which enables you to validate and adjust certain content and functionalities, followed by a wider deployment stage.

The beta or pilot stage

The best way to test the relevance of your dashboard is to deploy it, in a first step, on a campaign, country or specific initiative. As well as testing the technical functioning of everything, the most pertinent lessons are often related to the process itself and, in particular, the calibration of the correct functioning of the roles and responsibilities of the various internal and external contributors. It is therefore essential to test it in a limited way before deploying it. Once everything is fine-tuned and well oiled, it will be much easier to launch it more widely and maximize the chances of success of the dashboard initiative. So even if you are late in your delivery phase, do not neglect the pilot stage, as it can spare you many disappointments. It is also advisable to work in project mode, and to appoint a small steering committee, headed by your organization's KPI "champion." This committee can monitor progress and will be able to guide the necessary adjustments, in the pilot stage and after the launch of the dashboard.

The global roll-out stage

The learning and adjustment processes involved in the pilot stage facilitate the more general launch of the dashboard. You are now in a position to follow all campaigns by encouraging users to connect and monitor the performance of campaigns. Getting users involved is, moreover, the main challenge of the roll-out stage; the objective is to quickly encourage members of the company to use the dashboard regularly. For this, there is nothing better than arranging email alerts or sending out weekly emails summarizing the main results, with some comments. Even now, one of our clients is pleased that they followed this simple advice, because connections to the dashboard increased to such an extent that it quickly become an indispensable tool for the management of digital activities.

Key success factors

Constructing and rolling out a dashboard requires discipline and work, essential ingredients for its future success. However, some important factors should be kept in mind to ensure long-term success:

• *Relevance:* There is nothing worse than building something that is quickly denigrated because it is not suited to the users' needs. Consequently, all stakeholders must be involved, as well as committed to the actual development and construction of the content of the dashboard. Working in project mode, under the direction of a steering committee comprising one member from each stakeholder departments, is often the key to success.

- *Standardization:* A decision-making tool par excellence, the dashboard should be standardized, with the metrics and KPIs understood and accepted and needing to lead to the same conclusions. The challenge of standardization quickly proves to be a headache, when, for example, many countries or regions are involved, each with its own culture and levels of digital knowledge and sensitivity, which are sometimes widely different.
- *Breadth and depth of analysis:* If the objective is to monitor the performance of digital marketing, all paid, owned, and earned initiatives must be kept track of. The initiatives should be monitored and for each of them, it should be possible to analyze its performance and adjust and assess its relevance with regard to the objectives.
- *Speed:* It is advisable to take the time needed to plan and build your dashboard, just as it is essential to make information available as quickly as possible when in operational mode. It is difficult to make users monitor performance of their actions on a day-to-day basis if the tools available do not allow them to do it.
- *Profitability and ROI:* Never forget the main purpose of the dashboard: to manage the effectiveness and ROI of digital activities. Although obvious, it is vital to keep this in mind from start to finish. Accordingly, the steering committee should disseminate examples of best practice, where the use of a dashboard has been able to demonstrate or indeed modify initiatives with proven ROI.
- *Updates:* The steering committee should also ensure that the metrics and KPIs are regularly updated, in order to maintain their validity and their capacity to measure and explain performance effectively and accurately.

Incentives and KPIs

Sooner or later, indeed sooner rather than later, it is important to align the dashboard with managers' financial incentives. If the dashboard tool becomes central to the management of the business, it is natural that it also becomes central with regard to giving managers a stake in the company's results.

Realism

Be realistic about the results you expect from the use of your dashboard; a lack of resources is not an acceptable excuse. You must be "obsessed" with the need to measure, monitor, and thus assess the quality and impact of your digital initiatives. To do this, start simply; Google Analytics, for example, is a free tool that allows you to track your website. It provides a standard interface that you can adapt to your needs, its blog offers many tips, and its wider community is always full of ideas and ready to help. Learn how to align your requirements, budget, and resources with the anticipated results.

Key points

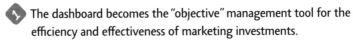 The dashboard becomes the "objective" management tool for the efficiency and effectiveness of marketing investments.

Building a digital dashboard involves four key stages:
- analysis of the existing situation, which allows you to align the necessary and essential KPIs
- clarification of needs by launching alpha or beta versions of the dashboard
- selection of the "right" technological platform
- construction of a user interface that will ensure the success of the dashboard

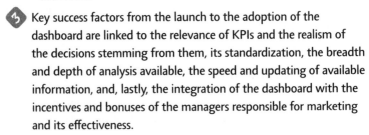 Key success factors from the launch to the adoption of the dashboard are linked to the relevance of KPIs and the realism of the decisions stemming from them, its standardization, the breadth and depth of analysis available, the speed and updating of available information, and, lastly, the integration of the dashboard with the incentives and bonuses of the managers responsible for marketing and its effectiveness.

Notes

1 See Davenport, T.H. and Harris, J.G. (2009) *Competing on Analytics: The New Science of Winning*, Harvard Business School Press.

2 Accenture (2010) "Onward and up: how marketers are refocusing the front office for growth," Figure 9, www.accenture.com/us-en/Pages/insight-refocusing-marketing-front-office-growth-summary.aspx.

3 In terms of the validity of the measurement, do they really measure what they are supposed to? The click-through rate, as we have seen, is often unsuited to attention/awareness objectives, for example.

4 WFA, World Federation of Advertisers, www.wfanet.org.

5 Extract from Davenport, T. (2013) "How P&G presents data to decision-makers", HBR Blog Network, April 4, http://blogs.hbr.org/cs/2013/04/how_p_and_g_presents_data.html.

6 Nichols, W. (2013) "Advertising Analytics 2.0," *Harvard Business Review*, March, www.marketshare.com/insights/blog/305-advertising-analytics-2-0-via-harvard-business-review. Nichols provides the quote from Nate Silver.

Conclusion and future prospects

As marketing and communications professionals are well aware, marketing has never been more difficult, but, at the same time, it has never been so exciting. If it is, and must be, in the service of the consumer, then today we have entered an era when this is so. Some authors and specialists even see in this a degree of "revenge" by customers, long treated "en masse" (in the sense of mass marketing) and in some cases, on occasion, "mistreated." The digital world, with its interactivity and immediacy, appears to be rebalancing the power relationships between the brand and its customers. More informed than ever, *customers have also never been so "resistant" to advertising* and its influence. Customers are now "mediavores," that is, they consume ever more media, but in an increasingly fragmented way. They are constantly connected through multiple screens (computers, tablets, and phones), and although their average TV consumption is not decreasing, their online consumption continues to increase, reaching a minimum of 20 hours a month in most developed economies and growing fast in developing economies. Ever more eager for interactive and social experience, customers immerse themselves in digital in all its forms. Switching from email messaging in favor of social networks, they become increasingly difficult to locate and reach; *the customer is a constantly moving target*. The exponential growth of mobile connections – for example, during the first quarter of

2013, tablets were the most popular connecting device sold, in other words, people now buy more tablets than PCs; and, in 2012, there were more than 25 billion application downloads from the Apple's App Store – has revealed a major trend that *brands must adapt to: SoLoMo*. SoLoMo refers to the social-local-mobile character of today's consumers: they connect with friends wherever they are, access information while on the move, and want information that is increasingly personalized and relevant, particularly in relation to their locations, desires, and needs. So should we give up? No, of course not, because although they are very demanding, these customers can recognize brands that progress and make the effort, and will respond positively to them with loyalty and by making recommendations on their networks.

Just as "Rome was not built in a day," so the marketing of today and tomorrow will not come about without effort, without trial (and error); it will advance through a series of successes and setbacks. The key is to try things out and to learn from what has been done by measuring the progress made, and its effectiveness, in order to better serve both consumer needs and brand objectives. *The watchwords "test, learn, evolve" should be at the heart of all digital marketing initiatives.*

In this book, we have tried to answer one of the questions that is on the lips of all marketing and digital professionals: what is the value of digital marketing, its impact, its ROI? In providing the beginnings of an answer, we first noted that it was a matter of "measuring effectiveness." Measurement imposes a number of requirements that must be met in order to move forward. Next, and most importantly, we emphasized that measuring the effectiveness of an action, whatever it may be, must be done in terms of clearly defined objectives and dictated by the objectives you want the action to reach. It is not measurements and KPIs that define objectives, but the reverse. It is from the objectives of digital marketing that measurement objectives and KPIs must follow.

We then recalled the AIDA model – the basic model of the functioning of advertising – which allows KPIs to be structured and organized in accordance with the objectives of attention, interest, desire, and action. Again, digital has its own operating levers, but marketing objectives have not changed fundamentally with the media. It is up to us to adapt the KPIs to the targeted objectives. We attempted to make an initial assessment of KPIs that can respond to the measurement objectives of each stage of the AIDA model. Indeed, "attempt" is the right word, because, once again, everything needs to pertain to the specific objectives of the brand and its market. Digital marketing managers need to decide for themselves which KPIs are most relevant.

We attempted to illustrate each major type of contact point in the brand digital ecosystem for paid, owned, and earned media (POEM), by reviewing the most representative contact points for each group. This part is probably the most open to criticism, and we invite readers to contact us so we can deepen our knowledge with case studies. By definition, the interactive nature of digital calls for constant updates and adaptations, and we welcome criticism and cooperation to enrich this book.

We concluded by recalling that digital is in the service of the brand and integrated marketing communication (IMC). We outlined the stages involved in implementing such an approach, the impact of which can only be beneficial, both for the consumer and the advertiser. Chapter 8 focused on the dashboard, the tool that can follow progress and the effects most closely.

Measurement budgets are not always available, but at a minimum, it is important to give yourself the wherewithal to achieve your ambitions. How do you show that an operation is effective if you do not have the means to measure it? How do you further optimize its effectiveness over time? How do you justify a digital budget increase if you are not able to measure its impact? Of course, it is not a matter of measuring everything, but of having the means to do so when the investment is sufficiently large, in comparison with other media, and to show the impact and the value provided by digital. Without this discipline, there can be no successful digital management. This situation and its consequences can be summed up by the phrase: "what gets measured gets managed."

The purpose of our approach has been to share more than 15 years' experience in measuring the effectiveness of digital marketing. This simple ambition is primarily motivated by the desire to provide a common framework for all stakeholders, so that the digital ecosystem can flourish in the years to come. Far from being exhaustive, this preliminary endeavor is, as we stated at the beginning of the book, a work in progress, not only because is it difficult to measure the impact of digital, but also because the environment is constantly changing with the emergence of new platforms – remember that only five years ago, social networks barely existed, whereas now they can account for more than 25 percent of the digital investment of certain brands – new advertising formats, and new forms of interaction, all of which make the digital professions and marketing in general both more difficult and more exciting.

As we hope you appreciate, this initial work is more than just a "user's manual" and can provide a shared structure for thinking about the subject, as well as the basics for setting up a truly integrated approach for monitoring and measuring the effectiveness of digital marketing. Once the framework is in place, it is up to the ecosystem's actors to appropriate it and adapt it to the specific needs of both the platforms and the organizations themselves. In this perspective, rather than revisit the AIDA model, we chose to construct and adapt this model's approach. Indeed, the persuasion and influence process has not changed with the Internet; rather, it is the forms of influence and the means of persuasion that are new. Understanding its functioning and its use by consumers should allow advertisers to conceive of their integration into a marketing and communication approach, along with the effectiveness monitoring objectives and KPIs that stem from it.

Although the journey is full of pitfalls, this is the price of the success that is waiting for you at the end of it. We invite readers to contact us, to share their thoughts with us, and to criticize. This will also help us to

progress. The past 15′ years have been fascinating, the next 15 will be even more so. It up to you and to us to make sure that this is the case.

To conclude this first collection of facts and thoughts, we extend our thanks to all those in recent years with whom we have worked, and who have dared to take risks: the customers of CRM Metrix, who have enabled us to get to this point, as well as all employees and friends of the company; and many others, including leading academics and practitioners worldwide, who have helped us to move forward and break new ground and, above all, gave us the energy to write the first edition of this book. We hope that there will be many editions to come, as we continue to explore the subject. A recent discussion with a leading ROI marketing expert[1] in Paris provided me with even more energy to continue the work. As I was elaborating on the content of the book and the state of marketing ROI measurement, I shared the fact that, in the current state, the book mainly covers micro-measurement needs and purposes, providing brand managers and agencies with an ability to track the short-term abilities of their campaigns to reach their objectives. There is room for macro-measurement guidelines, and although the topic is briefly elaborated on when covering the need for integrated marketing communication and digital dashboards, the net contribution of digital and marketing at large needs to be questioned and better investigated. To this end, executives and top management need to better value the net contribution of marketing and think in terms of ROMI, return on marketing investment, rather than ROI, where the "elasticities" of different marketing activities relating to investment provide a simple yet powerful ability to judge and value the net gains of different marketing initiatives. We are committed to further develop and expand our work in this area and invite collaboration to do so.

I would like to finish with a beautiful, well-known quote from Seneca, which I have often had occasion to reflect on over the years: "It is not because things are difficult that we do not dare; it is because we do not dare that they are difficult."

I invite all the actors of the digital ecosystem to dare to try and understand, measure, and press onwards. Let us be audacious together.

Looking forward to hearing from you.

Laurent Florès
@laurentflores (Twitter)

Note

1 Dr Dominque Hanssens, professor of marketing at UCLA, June 3, 2013.

Index

Printed and bound by CPI Group (UK) Ltd, Croydon, CR0 4YY